Family to Family

D1502917

Dr. Jerry Pipes and Victor Lee

Other Related Books Available:

Building A Successful Family
by Dr. Jerry Pipes

Becoming Complete
by Dr. Jerry Pipes

ISBN 0-840085109

TABLE OF CONTENTS

Foreword

G.K. Chesterton wrote, "The business done in the home is nothing less than the shaping of the bodies and souls of humanity. The family is the factory that manufactures mankind." Do you remember the first time you saw your child? I remember clearly the births of my two children. I wept with wonder to behold such a miracle. Then I trembled with the staggering realization that these little ones were now entrusted to my care for the next two decades or so. What a sobering thought! Perhaps like Marijean and me, you cried to the Lord for wisdom and help, wanting to be all that He intended for us to be as parents. In the following pages you will find wisdom and help to be God's best.

After all, parenting is a huge job. It is much easier to be specialized in the workplace than to answer all the questions of a curious child. It is easier to be the same thing to everyone than to be everything to someone. Home is where the tedious, frustrating, thrilling, and rewarding task of raising our children takes place. It is the stage where the drama of life is played out. Thus, home, as Chesterton said, "is a paradox, for it is larger inside than out."

At the times I feel overwhelmed and too small for such a big job, I return to God's promise spoken through the psalmist, "Blessed is the man who fears the Lord, who finds great delight in his commands. His children will be mighty in the land; the generation of the upright will be blessed" (Ps. 112:1-2, NIV). My primary need is to believe the gospel and live in response to God's call. The more my heart is captured by grace and delights in God's Word, the more my children will be deeply affected.

May the Lord use Family to Family *to open our eyes and soften our hearts to see and love the precious gifts He has given, and may our final reward be that our children have come to know, love and share Jesus Christ.*

STEVE GREEN

Acknowledgements

We are grateful to so many in the body of Christ for their invaluable contribution to Family to Family. *First, we will forever be indebted to Kenny Rains for both the inspiration for this project and the ministry evangelism ideas in Chapter Four taken from his book,* Families Making a Difference. *Kenny, you have lived these principles—thank you for sharing them with the body of Christ.*

Second, a special thanks goes to Tim Beougher, Henry Blackaby, Chad Childress, Robert Coleman, Phil Downer, Toby Frost, John Gardner, Sammy Gilbreath, Howard Hendricks, Wayne Jenkins, Alvin Reed, Bill Sims, and David Wheeler. Your insights helped shape Family to Family. *Those precious pearls of wisdom God entrusted to you and you to us are reflected in this volume.*

Third, thank you, Steve Green, for hosting the Family to Family *video—on a scale of one to 10, you were a 19. More important than your role in the video, thank you for modeling these principles over the years. Fourth, we are also thankful to The Larry Bateman Family, Ricky Browner, Cliff Cespedes, Paul Downer, Phil Downer, Glenn Gordon, Kim Gordon, Dawn Jenkins, Martha Jenkins, Beth Landry, Jeremy Maundy, Leon Maundy, and Sarah Maundy for sacrificing to be part of the* Family to Family *video—you did a great job! Your stories will inspire and help other families to become healthy, on-mission families.*

Fifth, we are indebted to the Family to Family *task force for helping us dream the* Family to Family *dream. Thank you Art Ayris, Karl Babb, Libby Bridger, Adrian Hall, Thad Hamilton, Debra Hochgraber, Wayne Jenkins, Don Lum, Mike Lundy, Tom McEachin, Phil Waugh, Ray Wells, and Kenny Wiggins for sacrificing your valuable time.*

Sixth, a heartfelt thanks goes to Richard Leach and Gerry Singleton. You each did outstanding jobs developing the learning activities for this process. Richard was also instrumental in proofing this material and making some needed additions to layout. Seventh, a special thanks to the Media Strategy and Publishing Teams at the North American Mission Board for doing a first-class job in producing the initial version of Family to Family.

Finally, thank you Bob Reccord and John Yarbrough for your vision for mobilizing families to become healthy, on-mission families. Your passion and support have made Family to Family *possible.*

JERRY PIPES AND VICTOR LEE

INTRODUCTION

Family to Family is for hurried parents who deeply desire meaningful family time, true significance, and long to pass the baton of their faith in Christ on to their children. Many of today's parents are experiencing

> **Family to Family is for hurried parents**

incredible frustration. They are busy and on the go. Running from work to school to church to ball practice to cheerleading practice and then there are recitals, rehearsals, business dinners—well, you get the idea. Sadly, in the midst of all this endless activity, 88 percent of those who grow up in our evangelical churches leave at age 18.

How do families get off this maddening activity-driven merry-go-round and on to God's best? The following story that appeared on the Internet recently illustrates a winning plan of action.

> It's just a small, white envelope stuck among the branches of our Christmas tree. No name, no identification, no inscription. I have peeked through the branches of our tree for the past 10 years or so. It all began because my husband, Mike, hated Christmas—oh, not the true meaning of Christmas, but the commercial aspects of it—overspending…the frantic running around at the last minute to get a tie for Uncle Harry and the dusting powder for Grandma—the gifts given in desperation because you couldn't think of anything else. Knowing he felt this way, I decided one year to bypass the usual shirts, sweater, ties, and so forth. I searched for something special just for Mike.
>
> The inspiration came in an unusual way. Our son, Kevin, who was 12 that year, was wrestling at the junior level at the school he attended. Shortly before Christmas, there was a non-league match against a team sponsored by an inner-city church, mostly African-American. These youngsters, dressed in sneakers so ragged that shoestrings seemed to be the only thing holding them together, presented a sharp contrast to our

boys in their spiffy blue and gold uniforms and sparkling new wrestling shoes. As the match began, I was alarmed to see that the other team was wrestling without headgear, a kind of light helmet designed to protect a wrestler's ears. It was a luxury the ragtag team obviously could not afford.

Well, we ended up walloping them. We took every weight class. And as each of their boys got up from the mat, he swaggered around in his tatters with false bravado, a kind of street pride that couldn't acknowledge defeat.

Mike, seated beside me, shook his head sadly, "I wish just one of them could have won," he said. "They have a lot of potential, but losing like this could take the heart right out of them."

Mike loved kids—all kids—and he knew them, having coached little league football, baseball, and lacrosse. That's when the idea for his present came. That afternoon, I went to a local sporting goods store and bought an assortment of wrestling headgear and shoes and sent them anonymously to the inner-city church. On Christmas Eve, I placed the envelope on the tree, note inside, telling Mike what I had done and that this was his gift from me. His smile was the brightest thing about Christmas that year and in succeeding years.

Each Christmas, I followed the tradition—one year sending a group of mentally impaired youngsters to a hockey game, another year sending a check to a pair of elderly brothers whose home had burned to the ground the week before Christmas, and so on.

The envelope became the highlight of Christmas. It was always the last thing opened on Christmas morning and our children, ignoring their new toys, would stand with wide-eyed anticipation as their dad lifted the envelope from the tree to reveal its contents.

As the children grew, the toys gave way to more practical presents, but the envelope never lost its allure. The story doesn't end there. You see, we lost Mike last year due to dreaded cancer. When Christmas rolled around, I was still so wrapped in grief that I barely got the tree up. But Christmas Eve found me placing an envelope on the tree, and in the morning, it was joined by three more.

Each of our children, unbeknownst to the others, had placed an envelope on the tree for their dad. The tradition has grown and someday will expand even further with our grandchildren standing around the tree with wide-eyed anticipation watching as their fathers take down the envelope. Mike's spirit, like the Christmas spirit, will always be with us.

This incredible story portrays what hurried, unfocused, activity-driven families must do to become healthy, on-mission ones. Mike and his wife organized and prioritized their Christmas holidays around a core value (to communicate and live the true meaning of Christmas), resulting in their passing that core value along for generations to come. Healthy families must do the same, developing a family mission statement and then organizing and prioritizing around it.

Family to Family will help you discover God's purpose for your family, develop a family mission statement, establish core values, make time for quality and quantity family time centered around God's purposes, and

> **Family to Family will help you discover God's purpose for your family**

equip you to lead your children to Christ and mentor them spiritually. You will discover the critical link between being on mission as a family and passing the baton of your faith on to your children.

These pages are full of biblical instruction. The bottom line—God's plan for the family has been revealed in His Word. Joshua said it best in Joshua 1:8 (NIV), "Do not let this Book of the Law depart from your mouth; meditate on it day and night, so that you may be careful to do everything written in it. Then you will be prosperous and successful." The success of our families will be determined by our commitment to know and live the principles of God's Word. There are many inspiring stories by the authors from more than 30 years of ministry to families. Additionally, there are practical ministry evangelism ideas and end of chapter questions and activities that any family can use to build these biblical principles into the fabric of their everyday lives. There is also a list of additional resources at the end of every chapter.

Family to Family is not a quick fix—however, discovering and experiencing God's best and passing your faith in Christ on to your children is worth the sacrifice. Jesus said in Luke 9:23, "Then he said to them all: 'If anyone would come after me, he must deny himself and take up his cross daily and follow me.'" This book will help you begin

> **│ *Family to Family* is not a quick fix**

or continue the sometimes difficult, but rewarding journey of becoming a healthy, on-mission family. Read the book together as husband and wife, or alone as a single parent. Pray about the adjustments God would have you make to get in line with His purposes for your family and then move through the process with your children. Thank you for loving your children enough to read these pages and begin the adventure of becoming a healthy, on-mission family.

Chapter 1

Healthy Families

It has been 12 days since Mom, Dad, Eric, Janey, and Melissa Morgan had a meal together.

No, Dad is not out of town, and no one is angry. They did not plan it this way, but they figure that is just the way life is today.

You see, Eric's bus leaves for high school at 7:05 a.m. Janey leaves for middle school at 7:40 a.m. Mom takes Melissa to elementary school at 8:45 a.m., then she's off to work. She works three-quarters time so she can be with the children—in reality, the only time she is "with" the children is in the van. She feels more like a taxi driver than a "mom."

Janey, one of the top acrobatic and jazz dancers in her troop, has advanced dance class after school on Monday, Tuesday, and Thursday until 6:00 p.m. (with an occasional Saturday morning rehearsal thrown in).

Eric's high school basketball team, off to a 2-7 start, is practicing overtime every day after school, except on days when there are games.

Melissa wants to be a dancer like Janey, so she practices with the beginner group, as soon as Janey's class is over.

Monday night is church visitation. Wednesday night there are church activities. Sunday night is church, too, of course. Almost every Friday or Saturday night at least one of the children is spending the night with a friend. And Saturday is lawn day, basketball games, dance performances...the list is endless.

This family has fallen victim to the American culture

Mom is taking a computer course on Tuesday evenings. Some of Dad's clients insist on dinner meetings. There seem to be two or three per week.

Perhaps you recognize this family. Stretched, stressed, and losing touch with each other. This family is easy to find. It lives in your neighborhood, on your block—maybe in your house. Whether you are raising your children with your spouse, are a single parent, or have not begun a family yet, you do not want to live like the Morgans.

This family has fallen victim to the American culture. American Family Association research shows:

◆ Only 34 percent of America's families eat one meal together each day.
◆ The average father spends only eight to 10 minutes a day with his children. This includes television and meal times.
◆ Only 12 percent of America's families pray together.
◆ The average couple spends only four minutes of uninterrupted time together a day.[1]

"The statistics also point out that although most adults regard family as their most satisfying aspect of life, they also regard it as their most frustrating!" writes renowned Christian researcher George Barna. "Believe me, we have a family crisis in America today."[2]

But why? Is there anything wrong with the above family's activities? The children's athletic activities are healthy, aren't they? They teach discipline, commitment, how to win and lose. Dad has to do business, doesn't he? And Mom, well, after shuttling the children to and from school and teaching them all these years, she has the right to take a class so she can refine something herself, doesn't she?

And you can't get too much church, can you? So what if Mom and Dad went to visitation and left Eric at home when they hadn't spent 15 minutes with him in a week; they were doing it for God.

The truth is that there is nothing wrong with any particular element of the above family's schedule. But collectively, it adds up to a family that knows what each other does, but does not know each other. It is a mom and dad who provide physically, but do not make the time to provide emotionally and spiritually. Each of the above family members is searching for significance—Eric through basketball; Janey through dance; Melissa through trying to be like Janey; Mom through working and caring for her children; Dad through providing financially. In the midst of it all, they have lost the significance of what God designed them to be. Their effort is individual and misdirected rather than as a family and Christ-centered.

This all-too-typical family is like a pressure cooker. The instructions for operating a pressure cooker might look something like this:

◆ Check pressure regulator vent and pressure indicator stem and safety tube openings before opening.
◆ For best results fill one-half to two-thirds full. DO NOT OVERFILL!
◆ Indicator stem rises when cooker is under pressure.
◆ When fully pressurized the regulator will "hiss and rock." This is normal and allows excessive steam to escape.[3]

Is your family hissing and rocking? Is it overfilled? Do you have a clue what the pressure indicators are? If mishandled, a pressure cooker will explode. If mishandled, so will your family!

This book examines how to avoid an explosion in your family by structuring it in a healthy fashion-the fashion prescribed by God—and applying its proper significance—the significance applied to it by God. The study will help you develop quality and quantity time with your family while helping you understand God's purpose for your family. It will also help you understand how to turn that purpose into action. It is not a comprehensive guide to every subject on which it touches, but a tool that shows you how to use other tools to set your family on God's course.

First, it will be necessary to examine your family. If it bears any semblance to the one above, you are not ready to be on mission for God. To proceed, here are a few suggestions.

Examine your family.

Is it a cohesive unit or a disjointed collection of individuals?

Is it on mission for God or unsure of its mission?

Is it flowing or fumbling? Disciplined or destructive? Purposeful or pointless?

The seven marks of a "hurried" family:
1. Can't relax
2. Can't enjoy quiet
3. Never feel satisfied
4. Absence of absolutes
5. They are suffering servants—great people, who do wonderful things for others, but are unhappy because they do good things for wrong reasons.
6. There is a storm rumbling beneath the calm.
7. They are "world-class" overachievers.[4]

If the above family resembles your family—if the above marks apply—what have you taught your children to do? Go faster and faster and see less and less of their family? It is time to reshape your family by God's design—and the good news is that He will give you the strength to do it!

Discovering real purpose and passing that purpose to your children will require making adjustments. For your family to take several steps forward, each member may have to take at least one step backward. What is good

What is a healthy family?

will have to be surrendered in favor of what is best. The "American dream" will have been reexamined under the light of God's purposes as revealed in His Word. If mother and father are working to provide the basic necessities, that is one thing. If they are working to get a bigger house, one more car, a bigger piece of the "dream," perhaps they need a bigger home and a smaller house.

More than at any other time in history, families are asking the questions, "What is a healthy family?" and "How do we become one?" It is crucial that parents learn to unify their family around a central, godly purpose. The family is under immense stress because it has no central focus—and that central focus should be Christ.

What is a family? God's original plan is for a man and woman to marry for life and multiply and replenish the earth. Genesis 2:24 (RSV) says, "Therefore a man leaves his father and his mother and cleaves to his wife and they shall become one flesh." This portrait is a lot more common today than the secular media would have us believe. However, perhaps due to circumstances beyond your control, you are not living in a classic family structure. Too often we think of family only in the traditional sense, but that excludes many. Most communities are made up of not only traditional families, but of single-parent families, married couples with no children, blended families, and single adults. For the purpose of this book, a family is defined as "persons related to one another by marriage, blood, or adoption."[5]

Henry Drummond, Scottish evangelist of the nineteenth century, once wrote, "The family circle is the supreme conductor of Christianity."[6]

Indeed, it was intended to be so. Deuteronomy 6 and the whole counsel of the Word of God makes it plain. Moses said, "You shall love the Lord your God with all your heart, with all your soul, and with all your strength. And these words which I command you today shall be in your heart. You shall teach them diligently to your children, and shall talk of them when you sit in your house, when you walk by the way, when you lie down, and when you rise up...You shall write them on the doorposts of your house and on your gates" (Deut. 6:6-7,9, NKJV).

Clearly, God intended the family to be the most basic social unit of society. Yet, many people today cannot agree on a definition of "family."

Phil Downer, author of *A Father's Reward,* writes, "Over and over we are told by 'experts' that the average young person in America has no picture, no mental or emotional image, of what a normal or healthy home is like. As a result of changing expectations, definitions of normalcy are changing as well. 'Since kids don't define "normal," as a traditional two-parent family,' the reasoning goes, 'why keep trying to preserve it? We'll redefine life's basic structures in order to meet evolving expectations.'"[7]

However, we do not have that option. According to Deuteronomy 6, the family should work together, eat together, talk together, worship together, and play together. The consistent, abiding presence of the parents is inherent in the passage.

If you are a single parent, the challenge is greater, but the mandate is the same. Indeed, it is important for you to identify same-sex role models for your children. These might come from extended family, close friends, or church family.

Furthermore, it is clear from this passage that the family is to carry the message of God's love. It says, "you shall talk of them (the words He commands us) when you...walk by the way" (Deut. 6:7, NKJV). And it says to "write them on the doorposts of your house and on your gates" (Deut. 6:9, NKJV). Even though this is an Old Testament passage, it is clearly an evangelistic one. The family is to make plain to those around them what, and in Whom, they believe.

Proverbs 22:6 (NKJV) tells us, "Train up a child in the way he should go, and when he is old he will not depart from it."

There is a crisis between belief and action

This is a clear endorsement and mandate for the parents to shepherd the children. A healthy family is at the core of this verse. That the family should be on mission for God is inherent in many passages that communicate specifically the heart of God, such as Matthew 25:31-46, Matthew 28:18-20, Romans 12:9-21, and Colossians 1:27-28. To be on mission means to intentionally carry His love and His hope to your family, friends, neighbors, community, and acquaintances out of the overflow of an intimate walk with God.

Many North American families agree with the principles of the above passages. They affirm "family values." Yet, they seem unable to live according to them. They agree that unbelievers should be introduced to Christ, yet they ignore their lost neighbors. There is a crisis between belief and action.

Says Richard Land, "The situation is so severe that there are now numerous attempts to redefine the family to fit its current dysfunctional and crisis condition."[8]

Instead of trying to justify the problem by changing the standards, Americans can solve the problem by returning to the original blueprint of the family. In the process, they can be part of winning their loved ones, neighbors, and acquaintances to Christ. They can find the significance many are searching for in the timeless, powerful truth of Jesus Christ.

Says Land, "I can think of few more effective witnessing tools than to have a happy, intact Christian family where the husband loves the wife as Christ loved the church and where he is providing for his family as the Bible commands him to."[9]

A healthy family is...

One that spends quantity and quality time together.

A healthy family cannot exist without time together. We must explode the myth that, "We have quality time, not quantity time." It takes time to invest in your children, and if they see more of their dance teacher and basketball coach than they do of you, then the dance teacher and basketball coach have the greatest influences. Fathers, in particular, must be careful in this area. Barna writes, "There is no research, however, that supports the view that the quality of the time parents and their offspring spend together is an acceptable substitute for the quantity of time committed to that relationship."[10] Please note the following study sited in a recent *Focus on the Family* magazine, "Dr. Blake Bowden and his colleagues at the Cincinnati Children's Hospital Center studied 527 teenagers to learn what family and lifestyle characteristics were related to mental health and adjustment. Their findings were significant.

What they found was that adolescents whose parents ate dinner with them five times per week or more were the least likely to be on drugs, to be depressed, or to be in trouble with the law. They were more likely to be doing well in school and to be surrounded by a supportive circle of friends. Surprisingly, the benefit was seen even for families that didn't eat together at home. Those who met at fast-food restaurants had the same result. By contrast, the more poorly adjusted teens ate with their parents only three evenings per week or less.

What do these findings mean? Is there something magic about sitting down together over a meal? No and those parents who interpret the conclusions that way will be disappointed. What Bowden's study shows is that adolescents do far better in school and in life when their parents are involved with them, when they have time for them and, specifically, when they get together almost every day for conversation and interaction."[11]

One purpose of this book is to help you structure your family according to God's purposes and to help you understand how to spend quality and quantity time together.

One in which each family member is committed to the other family members individually and as a whole.

Likes, dislikes, and idiosyncrasies aside, there must be a bottom-line commitment to love and uphold each other, to be victorious together in the walk through life with Christ. Central to that is an affirming and appreciative attitude. "We have to learn to build up people instead of tearing them down," says Christian psychiatrist and author Grace Ketterman. She believes the mutual support and encouragement will help keep individual family members from quitting.[12]

One in which the mom and dad are approximately equal in their involvement in the raising of children.

Barna writes, "By the admission of parents themselves, mothers are at least twice as likely as fathers to bear the sole responsibility for handling each of six key areas of childrearing."[13] There are actually "absentee dads" who live in the home. Don't become one. If you are going it alone, persevere; ask for help when you need to. Build a support system around you. This book is full of helpful hints that, if applied, will help bring meaning and focus to your family. The principle of shared responsibility is key for healthy families. At the end of this chapter you will find suggested resources that, if studied and applied, can make shared responsibility a reality.

One in which the significance of each individual and the family unit is found in Christ.

The family may be a collection of individuals, but at the same time, it is an interdependent reality. Before we can be truly interdependent we must first be independent. For example, if mom is codependent on her children for her own significance she will not consistently do what is best for them. If she needs their approval for her own emotional health it will be impossible for her to meet their needs. She would be constantly caught between her need for their approval and her desire to do what is best for them. Two codependent people in an interdependent reality are like having two ticks and no dog.[14]

Healthy families are made up of healthy growing individuals who understand who they are in Christ. Much of the struggle of American families is over a search for significance, a striving for purpose. Mom, dad, and the children are going different directions as they try to find their place in life. They are looking for significance in all of the wrong places. Like the Morgans—dad seeks significance through his job, mom through the children, the children through their activities. They need to find their purpose in Christ, not in the things of the world or religious activity. That is not a putdown of activities such as sports and clubs. It is an encouragement to keep them in proper perspective. To be successful, you must have a plan.

John Maxwell defines success as a) knowing your purpose in life; b) growing to your maximum potential; c) sowing seeds that benefit others.[15] The emphasis must be on relationship—first, vertically with God, then, horizontally with each other. If Jesus is who He claims to be, then developing our relationship with Him and accomplishing His purpose for our lives must be our greatest priority. There is a Christ-shaped vacuum within every human being. It is impossible to find meaning and purpose apart from Him. You experience success and significance as you grow to your potential in Christ and accomplish His purpose.

What does it mean to develop your relationship with Christ? There are six basic disciplines necessary for spiritual growth. Everything God will ever teach us He will teach us through one of these basic disciplines.

The six basic disciplines of growth to maturity in Christ are:

◆ Quiet time—starting your days alone with God
◆ Lordship
◆ Developing a powerful prayer life
◆ Personalizing God's Word
◆ Christian friendship and accountability
◆ Developing your ministry—making disciples and using your gifts in your church

Just think—everything you have ever gleaned spiritually has come through one of these in one fashion or another. Maybe a Christian friend shared a truth, maybe you picked up a great principle through a sermon, or maybe you read an insightful book. All of these would be an application of one of these. Healthy families are made up of healthy individuals who are growing in Christ. It begins with parents and continues as they pass their faith on to their children. It is not the purpose of this book to teach these disciplines. There are suggested resources at the end of the chapter for that purpose. Family to Family will, however, provide the solid principles you will need to pass along your faith in Christ (including the above six disciplines)—first to your children and then to others.

Let's apply John Maxwell's definition of success to the family. Healthy families are made up of individuals who have discovered their identity and purpose in Christ, are growing to their maximum potential in Him, and are sowing seeds that benefit others.

One through which the baton of faith is successfully passed to the next generation.

It starts with mom and dad. Proverbs 22:6 tells us to train our children in the way they should go, and when they are old they will not depart from that training. The verse says "should go," not "will go" and "when he is old" not "in all his days." These qualifiers tell us we cannot guarantee what choices our children will make. It is clear, however, that they are very likely to make the right choices with the right guidance, and the responsibility for proper guidance is the parents. Chapter Three is dedicated to a full discussion of passing the baton of faith in Christ to the next generation.

One that has healthy time together centered on God's purposes.

The purposes of Christ are clearly set forth in the Word. Perhaps it is no where more succinct than in Luke 19:10 (NKJV), where Jesus says, "The Son of Man has come to seek and to save that which was lost." The Great Commission also clearly communicates His purpose: "All authority in heaven and on earth has been given to me. Go therefore and make disciples of all nations, baptizing them in the name of the Father and of the Son and of the Holy Spirit, teaching them to observe all that I have commanded you; and lo, I am with you always, to the close of the age" (Matt. 28:18-20, RSV). A section in the next chapter deals with this in more detail.

Mom and dad are to lead the family to focus on and carry out God's purposes. Mom and dad should be active disciple makers and should lead their children to be the same. Disciples should be made "as they go" through the routines of life, always with an eye toward being Jesus to someone in need. Healthy families are on mission for God. God leads the parents, the parents lead the children, and the purposes of life are clearly stated.

A healthy family has a stated purpose, intentionally passes the baton of faith to future generations, and lives the Great Commission by being on mission in its community. It serves in and with the church in equipping itself and others to share the gospel. *Family to Family* will explore these areas and help you equip your family to live out God's purpose.

To help understand your significance in the kingdom, and specifically how mightily God can work through you, take a fresh look at 'The Seven Realities of Experiencing God,' from the work of Henry Blackaby and Claude King.[16]

The seven realities of experiencing God:

- ◆ God is always at work around you.
- ◆ God pursues a continuing love relationship with you that is real and personal.
- ◆ God invites you to become involved with Him in His work.
- ◆ God speaks by the Holy Spirit through the Bible, prayer, circumstances, and the church to reveal Himself, His purposes, and His ways.
- ◆ God's invitation for you to work with Him always leads to a crisis of belief that requires faith and action.
- ◆ You must make major adjustments in your life to join God in what He is doing.
- ◆ You come to know God by experience as you obey Him and He accomplishes His work through you.

Now examine the seven realities adjusted for the family:

- ◆ God is always at work around your family.
- ◆ God pursues a continuing love relationship with your family that is real and personal.
- ◆ God invites your family to become involved with Him in His work.

◆ God speaks to your family by the Holy Spirit through the Bible, prayer, circumstances, and the church to reveal Himself, His purposes, and His ways.
◆ God's invitation for your family to work with Him always leads to a crisis of belief that requires faith and action.
◆ You must make major adjustments in your family life to join God in what He is doing.
◆ Your family comes to know God by experience as they obey Him and He accomplishes His work through them.

Taking it one step further, examine the adjusted seven realities with explanations:

Reality One—God is always at work around your family.

God is sovereign. Nothing you do and nothing that goes on around you surprises Him. The circumstances you are in, and the circumstances of the people around you, are opportunities for growth and ministry. Look. Listen. Pay careful attention to see how God is working.

Reality Two—God pursues a continuing love relationship with your family that is real and personal.

Having created every member of your family as special to Him, God pursues each one, seeking to raise them as a father raises a child. If you know Him, God is not some distant being, but a real person living with you and in you in the form of the Holy Spirit. If you do not know Him, He is constantly seeking to draw you to Himself by the Holy Spirit. God wants to be intimately involved in your family's life.

Reality Three—God invites your family to become involved with Him in His work.

Jesus was sensitive to His Father's will and joined Him in His work. In John 5:19 (NIV), Jesus says, "I tell you the truth, the Son can do nothing by himself; he can do only what he sees his Father doing, because whatever the Father does the Son also does." He wants you to do the same. He wants you to be part of the harvest, part of the ingathering of those He is drawing to Himself. Only two things will last through eternity: people (see Phil. 2:9-11) and God's Word (see Isa. 40:8). Do you want to have an eternal impact? If you do, combine those two elements. You know the Word of God, and it lives in you. You know unbelievers, and you know that if they do not surrender to Jesus Christ, they will face eternity separated from Him. God's work can be summed up by this simple statement—our purpose is to know Him and make Him known. We are to grow to maturity in Christ by deepening our love relationship with Him and then out of the overflow sharing His saving grace with others. You can influence the lives of family, friends, neighbors, and even people you have never met for eternity. What a privilege, opportunity, and responsibility!

Reality Four—God speaks to your family by the Holy Spirit through the Bible, prayer, circumstances, and the church to reveal Himself, His purposes, and His ways.

If you pay careful attention, as mentioned above, and ask God what He is doing and what He wants you to do, needs and opportunities will become readily apparent, and you will be able to work with God in your family and in reaching your extended family, neighbors, and acquaintances.

Reality Five—God's invitation for your family to work with Him always leads to a crisis of belief that requires faith and action.

God has said, "Go help your neighbor clean out their garage." God has said, "Go spend time with the elderly couple down the street." You may not like the neighbor, and you may not have any idea what to say to them. You may not have any time to give to the elderly couple. So what are you going to do? Obey or ignore? Go, and trust God for words, wisdom, and time.

Reality Six—You must make major adjustments in your family life to join God in what He is doing.

The Morgans need to make major adjustments. Like them, you will have to choose what is better over what is good. There may be less time for seemingly good things in order for you to serve the way the Lord would have you serve. However, you can certainly find some relatively useless things to omit and save time. How much television does the family watch? Sports are good, but are the children (and maybe mom or dad) more religious about ball practice than serving the Lord? Be obedient and bold about making adjustments.

Reality Seven—Your family comes to know God by experience as you obey Him and He accomplishes His work through you.[17]

You want to know what God is going to do in and through you? You will not find out until after you have obeyed. Clearly, the American family is crying out for help. It is searching for a center, searching for significance—and that significance can only be found in Christ. Your family is the only place for your children to truly learn what their real purpose is in life. It is the only place where the principles of godly life can be modeled. It is the only place where the crucial need for a relationship with Christ that can empower them to live out those principles can be modeled. Chuck Swindoll wrote, "A family is a place where principles are hammered and honed on the anvil of everyday living."[18]

The place to start is with a "family mission statement," something your family can produce together to reflect your godly heritage and its inherent purposes and principles. A clear mission statement, used as the template through which your family views life, will keep your family on track, thus reducing stress, increasing productivity (spiritually and in the world) and bonding the family around the most crucial value of Christians—ministering Jesus Christ to others.

Remember, healthy families spend quality and quantity time around God's purposes. This is what the Morgans are not doing. Mr. and Mrs. Morgan are in danger of failing to pass the baton of faith to the next generation. We want to help you avoid the same mistakes by showing you how to purposefully spend quality and quantity time with your children.

At age 18, Dawn Jenkins is at that unique point where she can look back on all of childhood and ahead to all of adulthood. She was raised in a home where the family's belief in Christ was clearly stated and purposefully lived out. She has been on numerous overseas mission trips with her family and many other short-term missions in the United States.

"I've learned how to live my faith and share my faith," Dawn says. Since she has had these opportunities, she can teach her children the way her parents taught her. To have seen so many people come to Christ is amazing—she would not have wanted to be raised any other way.

Steps to Making it Yours

Family Readiness Questions

There is a time for everything. You began by reading the book. Now to help gather your thoughts, review what you have read by answering the Family Readiness Questions.

1.   What is the first step to a healthy family?

2.   What are the seven marks of a hurried family? Circle the ones that appear true for your family.

* Can't _____
* Can't enjoy _____
* Never feel _____
* Absence of _____
* Are _____ _____
* Is a _____ _____ ___beneath the _____
* Are "world-class" _____

3.   A healthy family is:
    * One that spends _____ and _____ time together.
    * One in which _____ family member is _____ to the other family members _____ and as a _____.
    * One in which the _____ and _____ are approximately _____ in their involvement in the raising of their children.
    * One in which the significance of each individual and the family unit is found in _____.

* One through which the baton of _____ is successfully passed to the _____ _____.

* One that has _____ _____ together centered on _____ _____.

4. What are the seven realities for the family?
    1. _____
    2. _____
    3. _____
    4. _____
    5. _____
    6. _____
    7. _____

Family Applications
The second step in studying Family to Family *is to discover adjustments through prayer. To help you identify areas in which God may be speaking to you, work through the Family Applications. At the end of each, ask God to reveal any adjustments He wants you to make.*

1. Write out the weekly schedule for each family member. Include all activities, meals, sleep, work, school, and church. Consider using an interview format—have the children interview the parents and vice versa. Analyze how many activities are done as a family and look for ways to increase that number. Also, look at areas where your family is spending the most time. Try to eliminate one activity from each family member's list and use that extra time for additional family activities.

2. Most adults regard the family as the most satisfying and most frustrating aspect of life. Parents, list the five most satisfying areas of your family. Tell about an incident when you were frustrated. Be sure to tell about your emotions during that time.

3. Read Deuteronomy 6:6-9 aloud. What principles do you find? Talk about ways your family is living out the principles in those verses.

Discuss ways to live out those areas your family has not been doing.

4. First Peter 2:9 tells us we are His chosen and special people. Consider this as an opportunity to encourage one another. Write each family member's name on a sheet of paper and tape the paper on a door or wall. Write as many qualities under each name, other than your own, that you think makes that person special.

5. Explain why you think it is important for Jesus to be the head of your home.

Family Building Activities
The activities allow your family to experience the results of the adjustments you are making. As you select several and carry them out, talk about what God is doing in the life of your family. These activities are not an end unto themselves; they create a teachable moment.

1. Plan, prepare, and eat a meal together. Below is a suggested one-pot meal.

    Beef Noodle Soup
    1 pound lean ground beef
    1 small onion, diced
    1 package oriental noodles with beef flavoring packet
    4 cups beef broth
    1 cup water
    1 (10 ounce) package frozen mixed vegetables
    1/4 cup sliced celery
    2 tablespoons soy sauce

Brown ground beef with onion; drain excess fat. Set aside. Break up noodles in large saucepan, sprinkling flavoring packet over noodles. Add remaining ingredients. Bring to a boil. Add beef mixture. Reduce heat; simmer 5 minutes or until vegetables are tender crisp. Makes six servings.

2. Set a time to pray together as a family. If your family already prays at mealtime, add other times such as bedtime or when facing a decision.

3. For the next two weeks, spend quality and quantity time with each child doing something that child enjoys. Each parent should do this. If there are no children in the home, each spouse should turn their attention to the other. If there are other family members in the home, such as parents, include them in the process.

4. Schedule a parents' night out. Arrange for a sitter, and have that much-needed date.

5. Play a game together. Consider a board game or puzzle. If the weather is nice, go outside and play together as a family.

Scripture

The following verses were found in the first chapter of Family to Family. *For further application you could allow each family member to choose the verse or passage that meant the most to them and allow them to tell why.*

Genesis 2:24	Luke 19:10
Deuteronomy 6:6-9	Romans 12:9-21
Proverbs 22:6	Colossians 1:27-28
Isaiah 40:8	1 Peter 2:9
Matthew 25:31-46	Philippians 2:9-11
Matthew 28:18-20	

Additional Resources:

Henry T. Blackaby and Claude V. King, *Experiencing God: How to Live the Full Adventure of Knowing and Doing the Will of God*, (Nashville: Broadman & Holman Publishers, 1994).

Dixie Ruth Crase and Arthur H. Criscoe, *Parenting By Grace*, (Nashville: LifeWay Press, 1986).

James Dobson, *Parenting Isn't for Cowards*, (Dallas: Word Publishing, 1997).

John C. Maxwell, *The Success Journey: The Process of Living Your Dreams*, (Chicago: Thomas Nelson Publishers, 1997).

Gary Smalley, *Making Love Last Forever*, (Dallas: Word Publishing, 1996).

Chapter 2

Developing a Mission Statement

Joey's friends are sitting in the car, honking the horn, and yelling obnoxiously, "Come on Joey, let's go! You don't need that garbage anymore."

Joey, 17, stands literally on the threshold of the home where he has grown up, his bags under one arm, his other arm around his crying mother. Dad is in the foyer, hands on hips, with a look that shares anger and hurt. "You KNOW this is wrong, Joey. You KNOW. You're going to get yourself killed with those crazy people!"

"They're not crazy; they're my friends, Dad! I'm sorry. Maybe I'll come back. Maybe I'll go to college. Maybe . . . I don't know. Mom, let go. I'll call. I'm sorry."

Joey pulls away from his mother, gives his father one last, desperate glance, and races—as unsure of himself as he's ever been, but unable to stop—toward the carload of buddies. "The rules at home choke me," he thinks as he throws his stuff in the trunk. "I've got to make it on my own. I can't be what they want me to be. It'll be okay if I get past today."

Joey jumps in the back seat. "All right! Good move," Joey's new friend, Ramon, says as he pulls a beer out of a bag. "This one's on me." And they drive away.

Joey's purpose is at odds with that of his parents. But was his families' purpose ever stated? When Joey went searching for significance and purpose, did he have a lifetime of godly, directed experience to draw from, or a disjointed set of ideas that lacked cohesiveness?

You cannot totally guarantee that one or more of your children will not rebel. However, you can decrease the chances of it happening, as well as give them a firm foundation to return to "when they are old," by developing a family mission statement and then organizing and prioritizing around it.

Discovering real purpose involves making choices—choices about who you are and what you stand for. Joshua made such choices, and he announced them boldly, as recorded in Joshua 24:15 (NKJV), "And if it seems evil to you to serve the Lord, choose for yourselves this day whom you will serve . . . But as for me and my house, we will serve the Lord."

Note that Joshua included himself and his "house" in the declaration. He intentionally influenced those immediately around him to serve Christ. And what affect did this influence have?

It was Joshua, Moses' successor, who led the people into the Promised Land. This quiet, unassuming man had tremendous responsibilities, but he was not overwhelmed because he had a stated purpose, a goal, a mission statement. Joshua 24:31 (NKJV) tells us, "Israel served the Lord all the days of Joshua, and all the days of the elders who outlived Joshua, who had known all the works of the Lord, which He had done for Israel."

Joshua was a man on mission for God. His determined, purposeful intention to serve the Lord resulted in Israel serving the Lord. Joshua's influence rested on Israel for years to come as the leaders whom he had nurtured continued serving the Lord and led Israel to do so.

In a chapter of *The Heritage* aptly titled, "We All Wear Hand-Me-Downs," J. Otis Ledbetter and Kurt Bruner wrote, "The impact of our ancestral links often reaches across three, four, or even five generations. Those connections may dictate many of the patterns and expectations we carry through life."[19]

Consider the difference between the legacies of Jonathan Edwards, a renowned preacher of the eighteenth century, and the Jukes, an infamous crime family.

More than 400 of Edwards' descendants have been traced. They include 14 college presidents, 100 professors, 100 ministers, more than 100 lawyers and judges, 60 doctors, as well as many authors and editors.

More than 1,200 Jukes have been traced. They include 310 professional paupers, 130 convicted criminals, 400 who were physically self-wrecked, 60 habitual thieves, and seven murderers. Only 20 of them ever learned a trade, and half of them learned it in prison! Edwards and his family were on mission for God. The Jukes were out for themselves. Consistent with the biblical principle that the "last shall be first," the family that served others had more for themselves than the family that tried to take it by force.

The different focuses of the Edwards and Jukes led to far different results. You will want your family to reflect Christ for generations to come, to be on mission for Him. You will want your family to intentionally share the love of Jesus and the way of eternal life through Him.

Ledbetter and Bruner write, "The number one reason we fail to give a solid heritage is negligence—we neglect to create a plan for doing so."[20]

Clearly, you must be intentional about submitting to Christ as the center of your family. A family mission statement will serve as a centerline and guardrails for your family on the road through life. You may not know exactly how the road is

| *A family mission statment will serve as a centerline*

going to turn, but you will know when and if you have strayed from the centerline of your faith. When life is foggy, you will have a centerline on which to focus.

A family mission statement is a way for a healthy family to make Christ's priorities its priorities. What is most important? Why is it most important?

Raymond and Christy have just graduated from college, married, and moved to a large urban area for new jobs. As schoolteachers, the starting pay is not very high, and they want to save in anticipation of having a family, so they take an inexpensive apartment. Christy gets home every day about 3:30 p.m., while Raymond stays late to coach football. She notices that each afternoon there are hordes of children, some as young as six, seemingly on their own until their parents—often just a mom—get home. Remembering part of the mission statement she and Raymond have chosen, which includes the phrase "to show the grace and mercy of Jesus to those in our neighborhood," Christy decides to look for an opening for ministering to the children.

One day some of the children cannot go home because the exterminator has sprayed their apartments for bugs. Christy invites them over. That little gesture is all it took. Soon Raymond and Christy's home is the place to hang out after school.

The children help Christy make desserts and cook dinner. She occasionally helps with homework or comforts a child whose parents are having domestic problems. The love of Jesus is shared—by example and through words. In the two years Raymond and Christy live there, numerous seeds of eternal salvation are planted and several children—and parents—are led to Christ.

Christy was compelled by her priorities to inconvenience herself for the sake of sharing the love of Christ with the children. She understood her primary purpose.

Perhaps you have seen the illustration of the big rocks and the little rocks. A man wanted to get all of his rocks—large and small—into a widemouthed glass jar. He put in the little rocks first, then tried to squeeze in the big rocks. Not all of the rocks fit.

Emptying the jar, the man tried putting the big rocks in first. Then the little rocks filtered down nicely in the spaces between the big rocks. All the rocks fit.

As a family, you must determine what are your "big rocks" and "little rocks." You do not want the priorities of life to be crowded out by less important issues. Thus you need a family mission statement. Derrick Mueller, director of youth ministries and seminars at Bethany Bible Institute, says, "Husbands and wives, parents and grandparents, need to develop a goal, a 'blueprint' for their families—in the same way that they have a blueprint for the construction of their houses. Our 'blueprint' should take into account the biblical principles we value and combine them with our dreams and expectations for our homes.

"People who live together do better when they agree on a common purpose. A family mission statement is essentially a declaration of what each member of your family agrees to live by."[21]

Henry Blackaby, author of *Experiencing God,* reminds us that the family mission starts with

Family mission starts with the parents

the parents. He quotes Deuteronomy 6:6 (NKJV): "And these words which I command you today shall be in your heart." Says Blackaby, "I really think the heartbeat of family evangelism is with the parents. They've got to model it as a way of life." [22] Blackaby's five grown children are all active in full-time ministry.

A family mission statement must not be just a set of words, but a description of a lifestyle—one that is consistent with and reflective of the Word of God. If you serve Christ, you serve His purposes.

Jesus' Mission, Our Purpose

As you begin to carefully consider your family's mission, it will serve you well to consider the mission of Jesus, then to consider Jesus' directions to humanity.

John 17:20-26 (NIV) clearly shows that the purposes of God, Christ, and Christians should align to the extent that humans are capable of carrying out His purposes.

A verse-by-verse review of the words of Jesus in the four Gospels reveals at least 35 statements that could be construed as statements of purpose. Three of them are overarching.

Luke 19:10 (NKJV) states, "For the Son of Man has come to seek and to save that which was lost." This passage gives us two crucial elements of Jesus' purpose. The first was to seek. That is, Jesus sought after—went to—the lost. We see this throughout His journeys. Jesus did not sit still, instead as He traveled, He shared the gospel wherever He went. He went places where a Jew was not supposed to go, such as Samaria, where He shared the good news with the woman at the well. The second element to Jesus' purpose was to save. Jesus was the sacrifice for our sins, the means of salvation, "the way, the truth, and the life" according to John 14:6 (NKJV). This verse may be the clearest, most comprehensive, statement of purpose made by Jesus. All others are able to fit under its elements of seeking and saving.

John 18:37 (NKJV) says, "For this cause I was born, and for this cause I have come into the world, that I should bear witness to the truth. Everyone who is of the truth hears My voice." The statement, "For this cause I was born" leaves no doubt this is a mission statement. Though a broad one, it is important, because it stresses Jesus' overarching purpose to "bear witness to the truth."

Another statement of purpose is Matthew 20:28 (NKJV), "Just as the Son of Man did not come to be served, but to serve, and to give His life a ransom for many." When Jesus sought people, He served them. He showed them gentleness, love, grace, and mercy. He endeared them to Himself by His service. He set the example that others should serve. You and your family will want to serve others with the same attributes.

Jesus' ultimate act of service was to give His perfect life for the filthy lives of the rest of humanity, thus He was the ransom for as many as would believe on Him. We cannot do the same, of course, but we—through our actions and words—point others to the One who did.

Examination of other statements of purpose by Jesus (including Matt. 4:19, 5:17, 9:13b, 10:34b, 11:28-30; Luke 4:18-19, 12:8-9; John 6:38-40) reveals a cumulative list of the purposes of Christ: Do the will of the Father, bear witness to the truth, seek, serve, preach, teach others to evangelize, heal, fulfill the Law, separate holiness and sinfulness, provide rest for those who follow Him, be a ransom, call to repentance, represent man before God the Father, and save.

While you will not likely include all of these elements in your family mission statement, a study of Jesus' purposes should serve to frame your statement. Use these purposes as a test to measure your statement as it is being built.

From Jesus' purpose we naturally move to Jesus' commands. The Great Commission is found clearly in five places, not by chance in each of the Gospels and Acts (see Matt. 28:18-20; Mark 16:15; Luke 24:47-48; John 20:21; Acts 1:8).

A composite "Great Commission" can be made by a careful look at the elements present in each of these passages.

Matthew 28:18-20 (NIV), "Then Jesus came to them and said, 'All authority in heaven and on earth has been given to me. Therefore go and make disciples of all nations, baptizing them in the name of the Father and of the Son and of the Holy Spirit, and teaching them to obey everything I have commanded you. And surely I am with you always, to the very end of the age.'" This is the most quoted, the "flagship" Great Commission passage, and rightly so, due to its comprehensive nature. Found here are at least five foundational elements. First, and most crucial, is the authority of Jesus. If we are to storm the gates of hell with the good news of Jesus

Christ, if we are to interact with hurting, desperate, lost people, our authority must come from One greater than that of any man. And it does! "All authority" has been granted Jesus "in heaven and on earth." In heaven, to allow humanity entrance; on earth, to draw humanity to Himself and to empower us to lead others to Him. Verse 18 is followed by the linking term "therefore" which indicates its importance to the statement that follows in verse 19, " . . . go and make disciples of all nations."

Making disciples is the second element. This means much more than leading people to conversion; it means training them how to live as Christ lived, to walk with Him. This is clear in the command—which fits within discipleship—to teach Christians to "obey everything I have commanded you."

The third element is the comprehensive nature of the call to teach "all nations." There are no limitations in this world to our responsibility—indeed, our privilege—to share this message.

Fourth, we see the command to baptize the new believers. Baptism is a public acknowledgment of Jesus Christ as our Lord, and we cannot expect to witness to all the nations if we are unwilling to publicly proclaim Him.

Fifth, we are encouraged, comforted, and empowered by the promise of the eternal presence of God. He—Jesus Christ—is literally with the believer (through the Holy Spirit and by His sovereign hand) through every experience of life. This is never more crucial than in the witnessing encounter. What comfort—what power—to know that no matter how naturally uncomfortable the engagement, the Lord of lords and King of kings will give us the right words and affect the heart and mind of the lost hearer.

The second Great Commission passage is Mark 16:15 (NIV), "He said to them, 'Go into all the world and preach the good news to all creation.'" This succinct command leaves no doubt what we are to do, and it reiterates the comprehensive nature of the command— "All" the nations, "all" creation.

Mark 16:15 adds the command to "preach" the good news to all. It encourages the Christian to be direct in verbally communicating the good news. Delivery of the good news is expected of a disciple.

Luke 24:47-48 (NIV) is the third Great Commission passage. "Repentance and forgiveness of sins will be preached in his name to all nations, beginning at Jerusalem. You are witnesses of these things." This passage emphasizes the elements of verbalizing the message, the comprehensive nature of the call, and speaking with the authority of Christ. This passage gets more specific as to what to share, introducing the element of "repentance and forgiveness of sins." Note that it does not just say "repentance," but communicates the good news by stressing in the same sentence "forgiveness of sins." The authority of Christ is emphasized in a more personal way, noting that we are to share the good news "in His name." It is as if we have the signet ring of the King when we bear the message, we have His authority.

The Luke passage is the first to be specific in marking where to share the gospel, other than to the whole world. The words "beginning at Jerusalem" in Luke should be taken to mean that our assignment begins at home, in the household, community, city, and country where we reside. This passage specifies the element of the responsibility of the believer to carry out what Jesus commands. "You are witnesses of these things" can be understood—among other things—to mean, "You have the responsibility to carry out and carry on what you have seen. What you have experienced, share with others."

John 20:21 (NIV), the fourth Great Commission passage, far less quoted than the others, reads "As the Father has sent me, I am sending you." Perhaps it is not always recognized as a Great Commission statement because it seems indirect. Yet it is one of the most profound declarations in the entire Bible. It ascribes to Christians the conditions by which Christ came to earth. How was Christ sent?

> — **In love.** We are to minister to others in love, not brashly or with a know-it-all attitude, not as if we have attained something on our own and are now trying to pull them up to our level. In the love of Christ—with the tenderness and gentleness that He showed and shows us—we are to minister to others.

> — **As a sacrifice.** We are to sacrifice for others. To share the good news will require time we do not have, patience we cannot find, and communication skills we cannot muster. We must give ourselves away for His sake, and for the sake of the lost.

— **As a substitute.** Make no mistake, there was only one ultimate substitute, and in the matter of eternal salvation, only one is required. However, in an earthly sense, some are called to die for the cause of Christ. And when some die, others are frequently awakened—through the death—to the truth of salvation through Christ alone. In America, we do not think often in these terms, but there continue to be countless numbers of martyrs worldwide each year, dying for the faith, in hope that someone else, seeing Christ in them, might commit themselves to Christ.

— **In meekness.** This is a gentle strength. This is the definition of the demeanor of Christ. We are to express His gentle strength. We are to say what Christ would say, the way Christ would say it. Meek is not weak, it is Jesus.

The list could go on, but the implications are clear. We are sent out as Christ was sent out. He is our model. He is our companion. We must study how He ministered and ask Him to minister through us the same way. This element of ministering literally as Christ ministered is unique to John 20:21.

The fifth passage is Acts 1:8 (NIV), "But you will receive power when the Holy Spirit comes on you; and you will be my witnesses in Jerusalem, and in all Judea and Samaria, and to the ends of the earth." This passage introduces the element of the Holy Spirit's direct work through the believer in witnessing.

This overlaps with the element of having the authority of Christ, but it goes further to show how that authority is expressed through us—by the Holy Spirit. All believers have the Holy Spirit, the Counselor who will be with

We are sent out as Christ was sent out

us forever in truth (see John 14:16-17a) and will teach and remind us of all things we have been taught (see John 14:26). Our obedience to witness simply releases the work of God through us by the Holy Spirit. The Word of God is clear that only the Holy Spirit draws man and that only God can save, and that Jesus Christ is the only vehicle of salvation. This element of the Holy Spirit working through us brings the purposes of the Trinity together through us. We are Christ's hands and feet, His very body!

This passage furthermore reiterates and expands on the element of the comprehensive nature of the call. By stressing ministry in Jerusalem, Judea, Samaria, and "the ends of the earth," Jesus is saying, "Do My work at home, locally, regionally, nationally, and internationally."

Indeed, a key point of the Great Commission statements is that we are to pass on what we have experienced—the saving grace of Jesus Christ. That is what *Family to Family* is all about!

These elements lend themselves to a composite Great Commission Statement: ***In the power and companionship of Christ by the Holy Spirit, and beginning in our own home, we will testify to what we have seen in Christ Jesus by going to all the nations and preaching the good news of salvation through Christ to all people. We will go as Christ went, teaching of repentance and forgiveness, baptizing those who trust in Christ in the name of the Father, Son, and Holy Spirit, and making disciples by teaching them to obey all that He commands.***

His was an evangelistic mission; thus ours must be as well! Our desire and specific intent must be to extend the kingdom of God by sharing Christ's love, specifically pointing to the way of salvation. We are to be a people on mission for Christ, a people living the Great Commission (see Matt. 28:19-20).

How to Develop a Family Mission Statement

With Christ's mission and His purpose for humanity draping your effort, you will want to begin the challenging but fun task of developing a family mission statement.

This effort may be enhanced if you have your own personal mission statement. You can adapt the following process. And how about your marriage? You might want to consider a mission statement for it. Again, the process below is adaptable.

To have an individual and/or marriage mission statement before developing a family mission statement will help crystallize the process. Furthermore, as your children grow you will want to encourage and help them make individual mission statements. Individual statements can more specifically reflect the particular God-given gifts, talents, and traits of a person, while the family mission statement pulls it all together in a team effort.

The process for developing your mission statement is very important. It is crucial that you not rush the process. Make it fun, especially for the children. Be sure that everyone is genuinely a part of the process—this is a statement you need the entire family to "own," to wear with pride. You do not want to send your family off into the wilderness of life without a compass. The mission statement—based on the Word of God—is the compass.

Mueller suggests a four-step process for developing your statement:

Step 1: Take a family inventory. Ask:
◆ In what activities are we presently engaged as a family?
◆ What motivates us?
◆ How would others describe our family?
◆ How secure are we in each other's love?
◆ What things are we afraid of?
◆ What is missing or lacking in our relationships?
◆ What is the spiritual environment of our family?
◆ What are our priorities?

Step 2: Consider your goals. Ask:
◆ What does our family stand for?
◆ What values do we live by?
◆ How will needs be addressed and problems solved?
◆ What activities will be important to our family?
◆ What is the desired outcome for our family?
◆ Is there a Scripture verse(s) or passage(s) that summarizes our intent?

Step 3: Conceptualize the statement.
As a family, we will stand for _____, living by the values of _____. Needs, conflicts, and issues will be addressed by _____. This is based on the Scripture verse/passage _____.

Step 4: Fine-tune and personalize the statement.

Write the phrase again, this time in your owns words. Each member of the family should answer, "Is there something crucially important to our family that is not included in this statement?" If so, refine it. Rework it until you develop a form and substance that will be appealing and meaningful.[23]

You should refine this process as God leads, but this exercise should lead you to a suitable process. The process is crucial to the final product. Before you are finished, ask yourselves, "What do we really want to last?" The answer to that question may be affected by the answer to a similar question, "What really lasts eternally?" As previously stated, the simple but profound answer is that only two things are eternal: God's Word and people. Does your mission statement reflect a commitment to invest the truth of Jesus Christ into the hearts of hurting people?

Children should be actively involved in developing your mission statement. The means by which they are involved should correspond to their ability.

- Use paper and colored markers with young children.
- Allow any child who is old enough to write his or her own mission statement, no matter how elementary, and consider it when making the family mission statement.

In fact, let each member of the family write a suggested mission statement, then synthesize them. If you feel resistance from children, go slow.

> **A statement you need the entire family to "own"**

Some warnings about mission statements:

Use Your Heart, Not Head

Blackaby says the greatest danger of a mission statement is that it can become a legalistic tool, a set of words that are only in the head: "A lot of parents have it in their head, but Deuteronomy 6 didn't say have all of these things in your head. Parents will never diligently teach their children until it is in their heart. You know it is in your heart when you do it spontaneously, without having to think about it."[24]

Reflect Lifestyle, Not Legalism

Many parents will have to change their lifestyle in order to instill the things of the Lord in their children, that is, in order to carry out their mission statement. Again referring to Deuteronomy 6, Blackaby says, "Scripture says you need to teach the children diligently when they are sitting in the house, walking by the way, lying down, rising up. Our parents are going to have to change their lifestyle because they're not home when the kids come in, sit down, walk by the way. They're just not there."[25]

Involve, Not Invoke

This cannot be the creation of just one or even both parents that is announced to the entire family. The family will not have "ownership" of or any passion for the statement.

Reap, Not Rush

You must take in what your entire family is feeling and saying before making the mission statement. Rushing the job will likely leave out something or someone important.

Instill, Not Ignore

Once you have decided on the statement, refer to it frequently. Use it as a plumb line for your family. It should be instilled in their hearts and minds—through the filter of a growing vibrant relationship with the Lord.

Please note that your family mission statement may need revising from time-to-time, according to the ages of the children, changes in family structure, and so on. Be sensitive for the need to review the statement.

Examples of Mission Statements

There is no certain way your family mission statement should look when completed, but following are some examples.

♦ "Our family will share the love, grace, and mercy of Jesus Christ with each other, our extended family, our neighbors, and our community as we go through life."

◆ "Our family lives to be the hands and feet of Jesus Christ, sharing His mercy and offering His salvation to all who will give us the opportunity."

◆ "This family will show love to each other through the traits of tenderness, mercy, grace, forgiveness, and gentleness. Our words will be uplifting, our tone encouraging. We will think of each other before ourselves. These characteristics will be carried outside our home as we share the love of Jesus Christ with those around us."

◆ "The mission of our family is to share the way of salvation through Jesus Christ with a lost and hurting world. We will do this by modeling a Christlike life first in our home, living the attitude and actions of Jesus before each other. Next, we will seek to build relationships with extended family, neighbors, and others we encounter daily. In these relationships we will model the love of Christ with the hope of earning the opportunity to share how Christ makes a difference in our lives, and how He can do the same in theirs."

◆ "This family exists to live the great commandments and fulfill the Great Commission, beginning in our home and extending to every arena of life."

◆ "Our family will work, play, pray, and study God's Word together with the goal of becoming Christlike and sharing the love of Jesus will all of those around us."

Healthy families organize and execute life's priorities around a central focus: their mission. Will you continue to be bombarded by opportunities? Yes. Here is the key question: Will you choose, prioritize, and live those that contribute to your mission? With God's help and leadership, any family can learn to discern the right choices.

> *Healthy families organize and execute life's priorities around a central focus: their mission*

Healthy families learn to say no to some good things so they can say yes to God's best. The stakes are high for your children. Eighty-eight percent of the children who grow up in evangelical churches leave at age 18 and do not come back. However, when their parents model their faith and are engaged in the harvest, the dropout rate is less than five percent. One of the keys to successfully passing your faith to your children is for them to see your core values reflected in your everyday life. If Jesus is who He claims to be (science and history prove that He is), then developing your relationship with Him and fulfilling His purpose have to be your top priorities.

If you follow a mission statement like any of the above, you will be on mission for God. You will be intentionally sharing Christ with unbelievers. Take the initiative. Begin now exploring God's purpose for your family and make the decision to allow His purpose to shape your priorities.

If You Are Starting Late

If you read this and say, "I'd love to start raising my family this way, but my kids are teenagers! What can I do?" You are not starting too late. Later than you should be? Maybe. But it is not too late. What do you do? Four principles for

> *The stakes are high for your children*

parents who want to lead their family to be on mission for Christ but are starting late:

- ◆ Take it before the Lord. Confess to Him any short-comings in how you have raised your children so far (everybody has them), then make a fresh commitment to the Lord to raise them to be on mission for God.
- ◆ Take it before the children. Using discernment, confess to the children that there are things you wish you had done differently, and then explain that you are determined to make changes. Wise, loving parents know how much good a transparent, "I was wrong," can do when spoken to a child. It might be necessary, especially with teenagers, to frankly discuss some of their upbringing in light of how it should have been.

◆ Discuss the concepts of a mission statement and being on mission for God with the children, then be sensitive to the Holy Spirit. If they receive it well, you are off and running. If it does not seem to go well, do not get frustrated. It may take some time.

◆ Live the on-mission life as a parent or couple, whether or not the children have bought into it yet. If the children see their parent(s) focusing on Christ and His purposes, intentionally sharing Christ with others, and living by a mission statement, they will see real change. The idea will grow on them. Win them with your actions! The Christian life is a lot more "caught" than "taught."

Steps to Making it Yours

Family Readiness Questions
There is a time for everything. You began by reading the book. Now to help gather your thoughts, review what you have read by answering the Family Readiness Questions.

1. Discovering real purpose in life involves choices—choices about ____ you are and _____ you stand for. What choices did Joshua make (see Josh. 24:15)?

2. Compare and contrast the Edwards' and Jukes' families in the chapter. How did the Edwards' family live out Joshua 24:15?

3. A family mission statement is not just a set of words, but a description of a _____ that is consistent with and reflective of the _____of God.

4. What are the four steps to developing a family mission statement? Who is involved in creating it?

5. A family mission statement should:
    ✔ Focus on the _____, not the head
    ✔ Reflect _____, not legalism
    ✔ _____, not invoke
    ✔ _____, not rush
    ✔ _____, not ignore

Family Applications

The second step in studying Family to Family *is to discover adjustments through prayer. To help you identify areas in which God may be speaking to you, work through the Family Applications. At the end of each, ask God to reveal any adjustments He wants you to make.*

1. What are your family's priorities? Which ones are really big priorities? Do they get the time they deserve in your family's hectic schedule? Are they consistent with the Word of God?

2. Using the four steps for creating a family mission statement described in this chapter, work as a family to build your family mission statement. Use self-sticking notes and markers during the first two phases (*i.e., take a family inventory and consider your goals*) to aid in the brainstorming. That way, you can rearrange them in order of priority and eliminate those areas that will not eventually become part of your family mission statement. Consider using pictures and symbols rather than words to describe your activities and goals. Once you have completed your family mission statement, make copies for each family member to carry around, and post a copy in a prominent place in your home.

3. Read Bible verses found in this chapter. Look for ways to instill them in your children's hearts (and yours). Discuss ways your family can live out the verses in everyday life.

Family Building Activities
The activities allow your family to experience the results of the adjustments you are making. As you select several and carry them out, talk about what God is doing in the life of your family. These activities are not an end unto themselves; they create a teachable moment.

1. Plan a family trip to the grandparents' or a relatives' house to hear an oral history of your family. As an alternative, research your family's history on the Internet.

2. Read the sample family mission statements found at the end of this chapter. Visualize them using pictures and symbols. Talk about how your family could incorporate elements of them into your own family mission statement.

3. Read *LifeMapping* by John Trent, Ph.D. (Waterbook Press, 1998). Work through the exercises in the book and discuss each chapter with other family members.

4. Invite another family to your home for dinner. After dinner, share your family mission statement with them and teach them how to create their own family mission statement.

Scripture
The following verses were found in the second chapter of Family to Family. *For further application you could allow each family member to choose the verse or passage that meant the most to them and allow them to tell why.*

Deuteronomy 6:6   Matthew 28:19-20
Joshua 24:15   John 14:6
Joshua 24:31   Philippians 2:9-11
Isaiah 40:8   2 Peter 3:9

Additional Resources:

Derrick Mueller, *The Family Blueprint: Developing a Family with Purpose* (Hepburn, Saskatchewan, Canada: Bethany Bible Institute, 1995).

Larry Burkett, *How Much is Enough? 30 Days to Personal Revival* (Nasville: LifeWay Christian Resources, 1999).

Rick Warren, *The Purpose Driven Life* (Grand Rapids: Zonderuan, 2002).

Chapter 3

Passing the Baton

Healthy families pass the baton of faith in Christ on to the next generation. It is not the church's sole responsibility—or anyone else's—to win your children to Christ and mentor them spiritually; it is yours. This thought strikes fear in the hearts of many. God's Word makes it clear that parents are God's plan for the process of passing the baton of faith (see Deut. 6:4-7). God would never command you to do what He has not empowered you to do.

Six-year-old Jennifer grabs her mother by the arm as she sits up from the bed after saying the nightly prayers. "Wait, mommy!" Jennifer says.

"Now, Jennifer, it's time to go to sleep," Mom says. "No more stalling. Sweet dreams!"

"No, mommy, wait. I have to tell you something!"

Jennifer's mother expects yet another declaration of her child's thirst for water, but she quickly learns of a deeper thirst.

"Yes, Jennifer, what is it?" Mom asks. Jennifer asks, "Mommy, I want to go to heaven when I die. Will I?"

If you are a parent, perhaps you have had the joy—and the small accompanying tremor of fear—of hearing these words. When your child begins to ask questions about heaven, hell, and receiving Christ, it is crucial that

When is a child ready to receive Christ?

you know how to lead him or her to make a meaningful decision.

Whether or not you know how to lead an adult to Christ, leading a child is a much more delicate process. Determining accountability is the major difference between evangelism with adults and evangelism with children.

Can Jennifer understand? Whether she can or cannot, the parents should realize that her questions are very encouraging. Jennifer is moving towards God and increasing her awareness and concern over eternal matters. Now it is up to the parents to make some careful determinations. All of Jennifer's life, her parents have been on mission to show her Christ's love and reveal God's plan for her life. Now, they have arrived at a time when they can begin to see tangible evidence of God working through them.

The inevitable questions are: When is a child ready to receive Christ? And, at what age can a child have a genuine conversion experience? There is only one determining factor—God's timing.

Paul Meier, Christian physician and psychiatrist, says, "I believe that some children can understand enough during the latter part of their first six years to know that they are frequently sinful, that they want God to forgive them, and that they want to live forever in heaven—and they put their simple faith in Christ."

Meier received Christ at age 6; Isaac Watts at age 9; Jonathan Edwards at age 7; Jim Elliott at age 6; and Corrie Ten Boon and Ruth Graham at age 5. But not all children are ready during those early years.[26]

Signs of Accountability

Here are the things a child of any age must understand in order to surrender his or her life to Christ:

- ◆ A child must understand the meaning of sin.
- ◆ A child must realize he or she has sinned.
- ◆ A child must realize he or she has sinned against God.
- ◆ A child must understand that he or she is separated from God because of sin.

As a parent, you can gently but directly explore these issues with the child. Do not feel rushed! This does not have to be resolved the first time the child mentions it, and the child must not be pressured or made to feel they are taking a test at school.

In order to determine how much a child understands, parents should avoid asking "yes" or "no" questions, should frequently ask "why?" questions, and should not ask questions with built-in answers, such as "You want Jesus in your heart, don't you?" Also, avoid "churchy" terms—the child may have heard some of the words, but they will not likely understand their meaning.[27]

Jennifer's mom is nervous, but prepared, when her daughter asks about heaven.

"Honey, I'm glad you want to go to heaven," Jennifer's mom says as she sits back down on the bed. "Why do you want to go to heaven?"

"To be with Jesus forever!" Jennifer says. "Mrs. Evans said in Sunday School that if we go to heaven we're with Jesus forever. She said the other place was real bad."

"What other place do you mean, Jennifer?"

"Hell. Where there's a fire all the time."

It is important that Jennifer's mom know what kind of questions to ask her daughter. This conversation is going well, as the mother is gently asking the child to explain her understanding of the terms she is using. Now Jennifer's mom will guide her through some key issues.

"Jennifer, why do you think someone would go to hell?"

"Because they sinned, Mrs. Evans said."

"What is sin?"

Jennifer looks thoughtful for a few moments, then kind of sheepish. "You remember last week when you told me it was time to come in, and I ran off to Martha's house, and it took you a long time to find me?"

"Yes, I do. I was very worried that you would run in the street or something. And I think you recall that I was very angry, too."

"I guess that was sin, wasn't it?"

"Yes, Jennifer, it was. I punished you."

"Yeah, I couldn't go out for two days!"

"And I forgave you. Can you explain what 'forgive' means?"

"Like we made up?"

"Exactly."

Jennifer and her mom went on to talk more about sin, about how Jennifer sins against God, not just her parents. The conversation did not finish that night—Jennifer was getting tired, and her mom decided they could continue the next night. Some of the questions Jennifer's mom could have asked:

How does God feel about you?

What is sin?

Do you feel close to God now, or do you feel far away from God?

How does God feel about your sin?

Why did Jesus die?

What do people have to do so they will live with God in heaven when they die?

After a good talk the second night, Jennifer's mom—now joined by Jennifer's dad—felt certain that her child understood what it means to surrender her life to Jesus. Mom and Dad ask Jennifer if she would like to think and pray about giving her life to Jesus.

"No, I want to do it now. Right here in bed," Jennifer says.

"Well, that means you'll need to pray to Jesus," Dad says. "Do you know what to say?"

"Hmmm." Jennifer thinks about all her mom and dad have explained to her. "I would say I'm sorry for sinning. That I want to be with Jesus in heaven. That I'll try not to sin anymore."

"Anything else?" Jennifer's mom asks. Jennifer looks slightly bewildered. Her mom and dad are not sure she is ready.

Then her dad says, "Jennifer, I try to lead our family according to what God thinks is best, not what I think. Mom and I lead you while you're a child, but God leads us. So who does that make the leader?"

"God!" Jennifer answers.

"Riggght. But, no one can make anyone follow God."

"I want to! I'll tell Him I want to follow Him!"

"Very well," Jennifer's mom says. "Why don't you pray out loud, and Daddy and I will be praying quietly."

Jennifer is a little tentative, but she has been praying out loud since she was two. Only this time, it seems like it is much more important. With her eyes closed, she thinks carefully for a few minutes, then begins.

"Dear Jesus. I want to be in heaven with You. I'm sorry for when I've sinned." Jennifer paused a minute and looked up at her mom and dad.

"That's fine, honey," her dad says. "Go on, if you want to."

"I don't want to sin anymore, and I'll try not to. I want You to lead my life, like You lead Mommy and Daddy's. Amen."

Jennifer's parents felt joy, pride, and relief at once that night. The next week, Jennifer's dad called the pastor and asked him the best way to explain baptism to Jennifer. Her dad understood baptism, but he was not sure he could explain it well. The pastor was a big help. A few weeks after that, Jennifer was baptized and joined the church.

A key to helping your child through the process of deciding to live for Christ is that you be well prepared. Review the above guidelines and be ready to answer your child's questions and to lead them into meaningful discussions that reveal whether they truly understand. Always remember to present the gospel simply, using appropriate Bible passages. Also remember that children learn better visually than verbally—perhaps, a

| *A key to helping your child*

witnessing booklet written and designed especially for children like "God's Special Plan," storybooks, or a well-illustrated children's Bible can be used.

Any gospel presentation should include the following:
1. God loves you—John 3:16
2. You have sinned—Romans 3:23
3. Jesus died and came back from the dead so your sin could be forgiven—1 Peter 3:18
4. You must repent and ask God to forgive you—Acts 3:19
5. You must ask Jesus to come into your life to be your Lord—Romans 10:9-10. "God's Special Plan" is an interactive witnessing booklet. This tool provides a colorful, illustrative, biblical, and clear presentation of the gospel. It includes a sample prayer to receive Christ along with suggestions for getting started in the Christian life.

Sharing Jesus with Teens

So what about those in-betweeners? Those child-adults called teenagers? One minute they act like a 6-year-old, the next minute they act like a 25-year-old. The foundational things they need to know to receive Jesus Christ as their Savior are the same as for children and adults, but there are some principles that will help parents more effectively communicate the gospel to their teens. They include:

1. Parents must have a platform of integrity and trust.

◆ Parents must display and live a life of no compromise in all areas.
◆ Teens easily see through the facade of inconsistencies.
◆ Teens want an example of Christ in their home.

2. Parents must have open communication.

◆ Parents must listen and observe what is happening in their teenagers' lives. This will build a bridge of trust and communication for just about anything. Some examples include talking about sex, dating, relationships, salvation, and marriage.

3. Parents must not remove themselves from their teenagers'culture.

◆ Parents need to observe what their children are looking at, listening to, doing with free time, and the way they are dressing.
◆ Teenagers have a need to know their culture matters.
◆ Parents should know what is happening in their teenagers' lives so they will be able to tell them about the never-changing, absolute truth of Jesus Christ.

4. Parents must make it a point to talk to their teenagers about salvation.

◆ This should be easy if a foundation has been built on consistency, trust, and communication.
◆ This should be a planned time or planned from a spontaneous conversation.
◆ This should not be an attack time or a time of "Bible-beating."

5. Parents should be ready for any response.

- ◆ Be ready for, "I don't want to talk about it now."
- ◆ Be ready for, "I don't need your religion."
- ◆ Be ready for, "I'm not ready for that right now."
- ◆ Be ready for, "I really want to accept Christ right now."

Resources you can use to share Christ with teens are the same as ones for adults—they are fully capable of understanding. Among the resources are "The Four Spiritual Laws," "Steps to Peace with God," and "The Road to Hope."

Mentoring Your Children to Maturity

Every other Thursday night Michael has a date with Nicki. Michael has a wife. And there are 25 years between Michael and Nicki. Yet, they go out in public and display open affection. Not only are they not hiding their relationship, they are flaunting it!

Michael is proud to be out with Nicki. He shows her off. He even brags to his wife about her!

Of course, Michael is Nicki's dad, so it is okay. It is more than okay, it is right.

On this particular night, Michael and Nicki have decided to eat at the mall food court and check out their favorite shops. Nicki goes with her father into the bookstores and sporting goods stores. Michael tags along while Nicki hits the trendy shops. Both avoid the department stores. "Too boring!" they agree.

Most of these visits are low-key with light conversation. Just "fun" together. But, occasionally, the conversation turns more serious. Those are the times when Michael, at Nicki's bidding, has the chance to make a great impact. She asks what he thinks because he has proven he cares. She listens because he does not push. Michael does not press Nicki on hard issues during these "dates." He is just there, available, "being Dad," living the way he lives every other day, but living it before his daughter.

Michael works diligently and lovingly at passing the baton of faith to

Nicki. He trusts that when the time comes for Nicki to run the race on her own, she will be prepared to take the hand-off. The baton of faith is to be passed from generation to generation. This is what the Word of God says in 2 Timothy 1:5 (NKJV), "I call to remembrance the genuine faith that is in you, which dwelt first in your grandmother Lois and your mother Eunice, and I am persuaded is in you also."

Paul was writing to Timothy, a young man whom Paul mentored. Mentoring was crucial in Timothy's life, both within his biological family as faith in Christ was passed down and outside the family as he faithfully followed Paul.

This biblical example is for us. As parents, you will want to raise your children to be on mission for God. You will want to set the example of faith.

Unfortunately, this has not been happening nearly enough in American society. As stated earlier, 88 percent of the children who grow up in our churches leave by age 18. However, that figure is as low as five percent when the mother and father have been modeling their faith and are engaged in the harvest.[28]

Howard Hendricks is perhaps the foremost expert on mentoring today. He says, "The truth of the matter is Christianity today dies in the first generation. The average parent does not conceive his role as mentor, as a disciple maker, and therefore does not function that way. The reason is that he has never been equipped to function that way."[29]

Hendricks warns that merely knowing what to teach your children is not enough—you must be an effective teacher, a mentor. "The greatest curriculum in the hands of poor teachers is disastrous," he says. "Teaching is not telling and listening is not learning."

Modeling is teaching. Observing, then doing, is learning. Lois taught Eunice who taught Timothy who became a great man of God. Lois and Eunice were mentors.

What is a mentor? One who walks alongside another, sharing wisdom, knowledge, and encouragement in a loving, transparent way. The purpose of mentoring is to help bring a person to maturity in Christ. You will want to be a mentor to your children; it is a crucial part of being a family on mission for God.

The Church, The Home, The Balance

The church can help your children, and it can help you raise your children. It cannot replace you as a spiritual mentor. Hendricks urges parents to carefully consider the role the church plays in the family. The church is crucial, but it is not to be misused.

"The average Christian parent takes their children to the doors of the church and deposits them and says, in effect, 'We want you to lead them to Christ, teach them the Word of God.' Then, if the children stray, they have a convenient dumping ground."[30]

Translation: Do not think that because you take—or worse, send—your children to church, you are "raising them up in the Lord." They will not likely be any stronger in their commitment to or trust in Jesus than you are.

> *Nine of 10 people come to Christ before they are 25*

"The church's primary task is to equip parents to be parents," Hendricks says. "Home's primary task is to equip people who will ultimately function intellectually and biblically in and through the church. So play it strong and loud. When it comes to evangelism, remember that nine of 10 people come to Christ before they are 25. The bulk of them come in the early years."[31]

Phil Downer, former president of Christian Business Men's Committee, reminds us that many Christians have the view "that kids have to wait until they're adults to be discipled." Wrong, he says. Many quality materials exist for discipling children. Do not neglect the second half of the Great Commission—that is, discipleship—whether it is with your children or with other children you reach through family ministry.[32]

Hendricks asked, "Why is it that kids come out of Christian homes, go to the university, or go to the Army, and go down the tubes? Ask the question, 'How many people has that kid seen trust Christ through the ministry of his family?'"[33]

Hendricks' point is clear: Your children must SEE what you are trying to teach them.

When Nicki and Michael get in the car to go home, Nicki says, "Dad, I have a friend at school that is getting in a lot of trouble his parents don't know about. I mean, really bad stuff. I don't really want to say who and what, but I know he needs to know Jesus, and I want to know how to tell him about Him. Maybe if I can do that, it will stop this stuff and it won't have to go any further."

Michael is tempted to demand to know who and what, but he resists. He quickly decides that he must affirm Nicki's concern for the friend and especially for his salvation. This is what Michael has been looking for from his daughter—concern for her friends' salvation—though this is not the way he thought it would be presented.

"I'm glad you brought this up, Nicki," Michael says. "It sounds like your friend needs a lot of help. I'm thrilled you are seeing that the issue is first spiritual. I'll be glad to sit down with you when we get home and explain how you can tell him about salvation through Jesus. And, I know you'll use good judgement if there comes a time when you should say who is in trouble and how."

Nicki knew she could ask her dad about how to share the gospel because she had seen him do it often. In the mall, in the neighborhood, wherever they were, Nicki's dad had a natural way of getting around to talking about Jesus. Nicki could probably tell her friend all he needed to know about receiving Christ without further coaching from her dad, but at this point she wanted affirmation and encouragement.

That's why moms and dads are there. That is why the mentoring role is so important. You must learn about mentoring if you are going to be a family that passes the baton of faith.

Key Elements of Mentoring Your Children

Key Element One–Modeling

You have to become before your children spiritually what, in your dreams, you want them to be. Notice Deuteronomy 6:6 (RSV), "These words which I command you this day shall be upon your heart." Students have, what could be called, a built-in "bunk" detector. When you say "A" and live "B," then everything you say ends up in the "bunk" category. Paul made the statement, "Follow my example, as I follow the example of

Christ" (1 Cor. 11:1, NIV). At first glance, that statement may cause you to think how egotistical Paul must have been. In actuality, Paul was a realist. He knew the New Testament Christians would follow him. The question was whether or not he would follow Christ. The same thing holds true for parents. Do your best, in the power of the Holy Spirit, to follow Christ. Then when your children imitate you, and they will, they will be imitators of Christ.

Key Element Two—Be there

At the risk of being overly simplistic, simply being with your children is a big part of mentoring. They cannot learn from you if you are not there—or if they are not there. In the illustration that opens this book, Mr. Morgan is not a mentor. He provides financially. He involves his children in healthy activities. He takes them to church. But, he is not with them enough to mentor them.

Jesus set the example for "being there." He asked the disciples to join Him, then took them everywhere He went for three years. They learned how to live by watching Him live. Jesus ate with His disciples. He traveled with them, ministered with them, even slept where they slept. They were more than a team—they were a family, a troop of men being trained to be like their leader—and ours—Jesus. The disciples heard the Master teach, but, of equal importance, they saw the Master live. Jesus told His disciples at the end of His ministry that they would be His witnesses because they had been "with Him." The Lord understood the Christian life is much more "caught" than "taught." He was there for them and they received His message and caught His passion.

Was it hard for the disciples to walk with Jesus? The bad news was that there were no decent roads, no cars, no airplanes, and no telephones to send word ahead that they were coming. It was a hard but uncomplicated life. The long walks between engagements made it easier to be there for the disciples. Life today is still hard, but it is complicated. You must concentrate on being there for your children. Focus, focus, focus. Children know when your attention is divided. They know when you are physically there but emotionally a million miles away. It is incredibly important that we follow the mentoring example of Jesus and be there for our children.

Carefully evaluate your schedule and those of your children, and make sure there is ample time to be with them when they are doing things important to them—basketball games, dance recitals, and so on. Then, make sure each parent plans time alone with each child regularly, much like Nicki and Michael's date night in the illustration in this chapter. Hendricks reminds us that when children are young, they need lots of little bits of time with parents. As they get older, larger units of time are needed.

Almost any time can be meaningful time. Families today spend a lot of time in the car. Do not waste it just staring out the window. There are many meaningful things you can do with your family in the car, whether on a long trip or a quick trip.

- Keep tapes or CDs of Christian music in the car. This will help make sure that what your children hear is wholesome. Also keep available other tapes with Christian material, such as Focus on the Family's 'Adventures in Odyssey.'
- Use the time to report on each other's day.
- For longer trips, take good books and take turns reading to each other.
- Play games like "20 questions."
- Use the time to take turns reviewing out loud the Scripture you have memorized.
- Be creative, but do not let driving time be a waste.

Phil Downer is a successful attorney who has been intentional about mentoring his children. Downer reports, "There are meetings that I've missed and conferences that I've turned down because I was with my family. It may have hurt my professional advancement, but I'll never regret a single moment I spent with my family. When I do things with them, it shapes them. In a small way, I'm helping to prepare the next generation of Christian leaders."[34]

Key Element Three—Affirm them

Too many parents (and their children) get trapped in constantly correcting their children. With children and teenagers, it will be easy to find things to correct, but it may take some mental and spiritual discipline to daily affirm the good things. It is worth the effort to try to catch them doing something right and brag on them. This affirmation should be verbal and physical, in the way of affection.

Jesus had plenty to correct in Peter. After all, he would deny Him three times. But even before that, Jesus showed great confidence in Peter and affirmed him, though He knew what he would do. In Luke 22:32 (RSV), Jesus says to Peter, "I have prayed for you that your faith may not fail; and when you have turned again, strengthen your brethren."

Jesus knew Peter would face great struggles, and would fail; yet, He affirmed him by instructing him how to behave when he repented.

Key Element Four—Pray with them and pray for them

If you want your children to spend time with their heavenly Father, they must see their father and mother doing the same. Teach them how to pray by praying. Teach them when to pray by praying. Teach them the priority of prayer by praying. Jesus regularly prayed for and with His disciples. Parents must do the same with children. If so, they will respond as the disciples did to Jesus in Luke 11:1 (NKJV), "Teach us to pray."

Pray as Paul prayed for those under his leadership. He said in Philippians 1:9-11 (NIV), "And this is my prayer: that your love may abound more and more in knowledge and depth of insight, so that you may be able to discern what is best and may be pure and blameless until the day of Christ, filled with the fruit of righteousness that comes through Jesus Christ—to the glory and praise of God."

In *Praying the Heart of God*, Ted Elmore suggests 12 things to pray for or with your family.

1. Pray for the salvation of your family members (immediate and extended). (See Acts 10 and 16:16-34).
2. Ask God to help you provide a nurturing environment that is appealing for your family members to come to Christ (see Ps. 78).
3. Pray for each member's spiritual growth (see John 15).
4. Ask God to develop within each family member the fear of God (see Prov. 1:7, 8:13).

5. Pray for wisdom, understanding, and discernment in choices each member must make (see Prov. 3:5-6).
6. Pray for discretion (see Prov. 2:11).
7. Ask God to restrict the activity of the enemy in the life of your family (see Zech. 3:2 and Jude 9).
8. Pray for protection, especially from the evil one (see Matt. 6:13).
9. Pray for the children's school.
10. Ask the Father to develop integrity in each family member (see Ps. 26:1, 41:12).
11. Pray for the glory of God to indwell your house.
12. Pray for broken relationships to be reconciled (see Matt. 6:12-15, 18:21-35; Eph. 6:4; 1 Pet. 3:7).[35]

Key Element Five—Be transparent

Mentoring your children does not mean appearing perfect before them. In fact, to give them the impression that you have no struggles with sin and no problems will push them away. Children may feel isolated, imperfect, and unable to approach you because they think you will not understand their imperfections.

Sensitivity must be used in this area. Obviously, there are some things you do not reveal to your children. But do not be afraid to drop your guard with your emotions and struggles. Your home, and their relationship with you, must be a safe haven emotionally and otherwise.

Jesus was transparent. True, He did not have any bad to reveal, but He grieved, and He expressed it; He sorrowed, and He wept.

Key Element Six—Empower your children

Do things "with" your children, not "for" them. Mentors help people accomplish their goals. Parents must avoid the trap of doing for the children all the time, instead of doing with the children and letting them learn. It may be easier to do something for them—change the oil in the car, build the school science project—but it will be empowering to do it with the child.

Jesus empowered the disciples. In fact, He said they would do greater things than He did (see John 14:12). He said that He had been given all power and that He would be with them until the ends of the earth. He sent them out with specific instructions and with the power to carry out those directives.

Key Element Seven—Make the Word of God central to what you do

Ask yourself, "Why am I mentoring my children?" The answer should be some form of, "To raise them up to be adults who glorify God by accomplishing His purpose for their lives." In that case, you must teach them what the Word of God says and apply it to their daily lives "as (they) go" (see Deut. 6:4-9). The essence of Joshua 1:8 says God's Word is clear, that the key to succeeding in life is to know and live the Word of God. In Hosea 4:6 (NKJV) the Lord says, "My people are destroyed for lack of knowledge, . . . I also will reject you from being priest for Me; Because you have forgotten the law of your God, I also will forget your children." Robert Coleman, author of many books on evangelism, says, "The Great Commission begins in the family." The Great Commission, Matthew 28:19-20 (NKJV), tell us,

> *Passing on your faith—that is what it meansto be raising on-mission Christians*

"Go therefore and make disciples of all the nations, baptizing them in the name of the Father and of the Son and of the Holy Spirit, teaching them to observe all things that I have commanded you; and lo, I am with you always, even to the end of the age." He sees the family as an example of the Great Commission.[36] God has called parents to lead their children to faith in Christ and mentor them in God's Word so they can in turn win and mentor others and glorify their Father in heaven. Passing on our faith should be a basic part of what you are doing as parents.

Charles Stanley suggests seven ways to pass on your faith:
    1. Pass on your faith by sharing basic principles (about money, God's guidance, and provision, etc.).
    2. Pass on your faith by the lifestyle you live.

3. Pass on your faith by persistence.

4. Pass on your faith by participation in other people's lives.

5. Pass on your faith by praising your children for trusting God (and they will be motivated to trust Him again).

6. Pass on your faith by praying for your children.

7. Pass on your faith by being willing to back off and refuse to bail them out of the messes they get into. [37]

Passing on your faith—that is what it means to be raising on-mission Christians.

The Ins and Outs of Family Worship

Exhibit A:

"Oh, no," Kelly and Marshall Jackson moan simultaneously as their mom calls them to the living room. They know what is coming. Kelly takes off the headphones and leaves her bedroom, Marshall abandons the video game in his room, and both trudge reluctantly into the presence of "Mr. Spiritual." It is time for Dad's nightly sermonette. "Bible study time!" Dad says with a sort of mock enthusiasm. Kelly and Marshall roll their eyes—did they catch Mom doing the same? Surely not.

Dad opens the Bible to Jeremiah and reads a passage for 15 minutes. Then, as he is prone to do without warning, he asks questions. Kelly is embarrassed and a little upset when she does not know the answers. Marshall blurts out, "What do I look like, a Bible scholar or something!?" "Not exactly," his dad says, "and you won't ever with that attitude! Let's pray." Dad leads, then everyone returns to his or her rooms. Kelly grumbles to Marshall as they walk down the hall, "Are we having fun yet?"

Exhibit B:

The talk around the Calloway's dinner table is an informal survey of each person's day. Six-year-old Brenda spent the day with Aunt Ellen. They watched a new children's video after lunch. She recites the funny parts, much to the playful amusement of her mom, dad, and teenage brother and sister.

Someone cut in front of Mom to take the parking space she was pulling into in the grocery store parking lot. "Oooh, I got so mad," Mom says. "I really had to check my tongue to keep from saying something that would be a bad testimony."

"I know how you feel," 15-year-old Brian says. "I was talking with this cute new girl at school, and Roger Jones cut right in and started acting like a big shot. I really wanted to tell him off, but I dropped it." "Good move," says 17-year-old Becky, "especially since Roger Jones is an offensive tackle on the football team." Everybody laughs, then Dad says, "It's really hard to hold our tongues sometimes."

He drops the subject—for now. When everyone is through eating, the plates are pushed aside as Dad reaches for the Bible, as he does almost every night after dinner. Taking his cue from the evening conversation, Dad turns to James 3 and reads the first 12 verses. He gently encourages his family while acknowledging his own struggles. Then he asks each person for prayer requests. It's Becky's turn to lead, and then everyone goes on about his or her evening.

Which of the above households would you rather be in? The stuffy, "religious," boring, and long-winded Jackson household? Or the lighter, interactive, relevant, and personal Calloway home? Which does your home resemble? Maybe neither.

Family worship can be a great blessing or a great downer, depending on how it is handled. But it must be handled. Born-again parents cannot have an on-mission family without regular time together reviewing the Word and relating its principles to everyday life.

"Family altar time gets a lot of bad press," Hendricks says. "You hear that it is boring, parent-centered. This is where creativity needs to come. Gear to the child. Every kid is different."

There are many outstanding resources available to help parents plan family worship time, but following are some myths and principles for family worship. The myths were adapted from an article by Robert Crosby, published in *New Man Magazine*.[38]

Crosby's Myths about Family Devotions

Myth #1: Family devotions must be just like a church service. Not on your life! Who says that devotional times must contain an opening prayer, singing, and a sermon followed by a closing prayer? Jesus certainly was not bound by such a formula as He trained His disciples. He used dozens of object lessons and teaching tools to equip them. When given the option, Jesus chose a good story over a course in systematic theology. Wise parents will do the same.

Myth #2: Everybody has to sit still and be quiet for effective devotion times. Still and quiet are not synonymous with toddlers or teenagers! Cultivate attentiveness and respect within children when others are speaking, but remember that those are not qualities with which they come programmed. Those qualities are learned and it takes time and loads of patience. The best learning experiences for a child are those in which he or she is not only inspired to consider truth cognitively but to demonstrate it physically. Be creative in your use of visual aids. Remember, children learn better visually than verbally.

Myth #3: The spouse who knows the most Scripture is the one who should give instruction. Many Christian fathers today either became believers after their wives did or have recently begun to take their faith in Christ more seriously. The thought of "teaching" a devotional time with their families makes them nervous. A man must remember that what qualifies him to lead his family spiritually is not the extent of his grasp of biblical principles but his personal faith in Christ and the fact that God called him to be a husband and father. Growing in knowledge or wisdom will help, but foremost, a man must recognize that God has placed him in his home to lead and initiate God's purposes there.

Myth #4: Dad must always lead the devotional time. Not necessarily. There may be weeks when the father is overloaded at work and he asks his wife to lead them. Or, you may be a single parent. You may choose to rotate weeks. There may even be times you ask one of your children to lead the Bible story-time. Granted, the story may be a bit simplistic, but its "depth" will be in the fact that you are training your child to minister God's Word.

3 Keys to Family Worship

1. Share God's Word and let God speak for Himself. Family worship should not be a teaching time where mom or dad shares three points and a poem. Rather, it should be a time where the entire family seeks to hear from God through His Word. Read a story or a parable and then apply it to everyday life. Following are some helpful hints for applying God's Word.

- ◆ **Keep it simple.** One key theme is enough to fill one night. If you have smaller children or a teenager, use the Good News Bible or the Living Bible rather than the King James Version (KJV). Children may not easily understand he King James Version. For example, Proverbs 20:30 (KJV) says, "The blueness of a wound cleanseth away evil: so do stripes the inward parts of the belly." The same verse in the Good News Bible (GNB) reads, "Sometimes it takes a painful experience to make us change our ways." Which one of those do you think your teenager or child would understand?

- ◆ **Make it interesting; communicate excitement!** For example, use contemporary Christian music as a way to bring God's Word into your teenager's life. This can be done by playing a song from a tape or CD, then discussing its message and looking at related Bible verses.

- ◆ **Never tell your child or teenager anything you can lead them to discover for themselves.** The way you ask questions during devotion times will often determine whether it will be a time your children find fascinating or boring. For example, if you had just read the story of Shadrach, Meshach, and Abednego in Daniel 3, which question would draw the most out of your child: "So what did you get out of that story?" Or, "Shadrach,

Meshach, and Abednego had to stand alone in their world in order to stand for God. Do you ever feel like you are standing alone? What does it take for you to stand up for God at school?" Take time to consider what you will ask your child. Try to lead your children to discover and apply the truths of God's Word through asking sharp and focused questions that draw upon your child's feelings, insights, and impressions.

2. Share prayer requests. As you share prayer requests, parents, please be vulnerable! Take the opportunity to share some of your struggles. For example, you could say, "I am struggling with my temper, I lost control at work the other day, I said some things that I didn't mean. This week I am memorizing Proverbs 29:11(RSV), 'A fool gives full vent to his anger, but a wise man quietly holds it back.' Every time I'm about to lose my cool I am asking God to bring that verse back to my attention—I quote the verse and then ask God to help me." What have you just accomplished? You have said to your children, "You know, I don't have it all together, I'm struggling just like you." They know that, but they need to hear you admit it once and a while. You are also modeling Scripture memory, which is one of the key disciplines of discipleship.

Some of you may have a hard time with being vulnerable and talking to your children about your problems. You may be thinking something like this, "If I share my struggles, my children will not respect me, I will not do that!" They will not lose respect for you.

There was a person nailing up a sign that said, "Puppies for Sale." He did not even get the sign up when this little boy was pulling at his pants legs and said, "Mister, I want one of your puppies." He told the little boy he could not have one because they cost a lot of money and he could not afford one. The little boy, not the least bit frustrated, pulled his hand out of his overalls and said "Sir, will 37 cents buy me a look?" The old gruff farmer melted and out of the barn walked Dolly, a beautiful white Alaskan dog. Behind Dolly came four beautiful fur balls, and then the runt of the litter. The little brown dog literally rolled down the ramp. The boy said he wanted the little brown puppy on the end. The farmer said he could not have the brown puppy because it would not be able to run or jump. "That puppy is crippled!" said the farmer. The little boy pulled up the leg of his overalls and exposed the metal brace on his leg and said, "That puppy is going to need somebody just like me who understands!" May I suggest that your children will never be perfect, and they cannot relate to perfection. What they can relate to is a mom and a dad who are head-over-heels in love with Jesus and are willing to share the struggle. Your taking the lead in being vulnerable will open the door for your children to share their struggles as well.

3. *Have a season of prayer.* Give everyone an opportunity to pray. While it may be more expedient to lead the prayer as a parent, your family will be drawn together as one as you lift your hearts together to God in prayer. The disciples requested of Jesus, "Lord, teach us to pray." Although they may not realize it, your children are asking, "teach us to pray." Family worship provides an incredible opportunity for you to help your children understand and apply what God's Word teaches about prayer. Share God's Word and let God speak for Himself. Share prayer requests and have a season of prayer.

You can do it. You can lead your children to Christ, mentor them, and lead your family in worship. God has given you not only the commands to do so but the power and resources. Take responsibility for leading your family to be on mission for God. Healthy families pass the baton of faith in Christ to the next generation.

Steps to Making it Yours

Family Readiness Questions
There is a time for everything. You began by reading the book. Now to help gather your thoughts, review what you have read by answering the Family Resources Questions.

1. What are four things about sin that a child (or anyone) must understand in order to surrender his or her life to Christ?

1. _____

2. _____

3. _____

4. _____

2. Match the verse with the phrase in this gospel presentation.
   a. God loves you.   ____1 Peter 3:18
   b. You have sinned.   ____John 3:16
   c. Jesus died and came back   ____Romans 10:9-10
      from the dead, so your sin
      could be forgiven.
   d. You must repent and ask   ____Romans 3:23
      God to forgive you.
   e. You must ask Jesus to come into   ____Acts 3:19
      your life to be your Lord.

3. What special considerations should be made when witnessing to teens?_____

4. Fill in the blanks on mentoring children.
   ◆ _____

   ◆ _____ there

   ◆ _____ them

   ◆ _____ with them and _____ for them

   ◆ Be _____

   ◆ _____ your children

◆ Make the _____ of _____ central to _____ you do

5. What is one way to make family devotion time interesting and exciting?_____

Family Applications
The second step in studying Family to Family *is to discover adjustments through prayer. To help you identify areas in which God may be speaking to you, work through the Family Applications. At the end of each, ask God to reveal any adjustments He wants you to make.*

1. Share your testimony as if it were a story during family time. You can read Paul's story in Acts 26:1-29 to help you develop your own.

2. Develop a mentoring contract with your children. Include commitments that you and your children agree to do. These could include how you will spend your time, how you will lovingly correct them (in private, not publicly), how you will both make mistakes (and forgive one another), how you will learn from one another, how you will handle conflict, and how you will have fun. Include space for you and your children to sign and date the contract. Place it where you will all see it.

3. Read through the keys to family devotions in this chapter, writing them on index cards. Discuss them and reach a consensus on the order of importance to your family (i.e., rank order the keys).

4. Talk about the significance of wearing Christian theme bracelets and clothing.

Family Building Activities
The activities allow your family to experience the results of the adjustments you are making. As you select several and carry them out, talk about what God is doing in the life of your family. These activities are not an end unto themselves; they create a teachable moment.

1. During family time, make an "On Mission To Share Jesus"

bracelet out of a leather shoelace and colored craft beads. Have each family member discuss a color's significance.

To make the bracelet, cut the leather shoestring in lengths to fit each person's wrist with several inches added to tie knots. The length will vary based on the size of each person's wrist. About six inches from one end, tie a knot. Next, string the beads in color order as indicated below. At the end of the string (after the gold bead), tie another knot. You should be able to hold the string by both ends with the beads held in the middle of the shoestring by the two knots. Tie a knot at each end of the leather shoestring. To wear the bracelet, wrap it around the wrist and tie a square knot to hold it in place. When placing the bracelet on children, be sure the string is not so tight that it causes injury.

- ◆ The first knot stands for your physical birth. God loves you and has a wonderful plan for your life (see John 10:10).
- ◆ The first bead is dark gray and stands for "O" in the word "on." This signifies sin, darkness, and separation from God (see Rom. 3:10, 23). We must admit that we need Jesus.
- ◆ The second bead is red and stands for "M" in the word "mission." This signifies Christ's blood and the forgiveness of sin. As Romans 5:8 (NIV) says, "While we were still sinners, Christ died for us." We must repent of our sins.
- ◆ The third bead is blue and stands for "T" in the word "to." This signifies that we should believe and receive Jesus and His offer of forgiveness and eternal life (see Rom. 10:9-10).
- ◆ The fourth bead is white and stands for "S" in the word "share." This signifies that we should celebrate the beauty of forgiveness and eternal life (see Isa. 12:1,2).
- ◆ The fifth bead is green and stands for "J" in the name "Jesus." This signifies growth. Be unashamed of Jesus. Confess Him publicly and follow Him in baptism. Study God's Word and learn to pray.
- ◆ The second knot stands for our eternal security (see John 10:27).

2. As a family, decide on a time and day to begin family worship. Brainstorm what elements of worship (e.g., music, Scripture, lesson, and activity) your family would like to have. Assign a leader for the first time. Make a fun evening of this preparation time by ordering pizza to eat during the discussion. Develop a family devotion calendar that includes the leader of the week or month, topics, Scripture, and other significant items.

3. Adults and teens should obtain New Testaments for each family member and turn it into a "witnessing" New Testament by highlighting the key verses to lead someone to Christ. Write the reference of the first verse inside the front cover, and by each subsequent verse, write the reference of the next verse. Have each family member practice flipping through the plan of salvation using these New Testaments. Teens and older children may want to use schoolbook covers that communicate the gospel. (See resources for information on this item.) Parents may also want to use the "God's Special Plan" booklet to witness to children.

4. Parents, go on a walk and discuss ways to bless your children. Talk about potential teachable moments that may arise during the next two weeks.

Scripture
The following verses were found in the third chapter of Family to Family. *For further application you could allow each family member to choose the verse or passage that meant the most to them and allow them to tell why.*

Deuteronomy 6:4-9	Acts 3:19	2 Timothy 1:5
Matthew 28:18-20	Romans 3:23	1 Peter 3:18
Luke 22:32	Romans 10:9-10	

John 3:16   Ephesians 6:4

Additional Resources:

Skip Arnhart, *Sharing God's Special Plan with Children* (Alpharetta, Georgia: North American Mission Board, 1999).

David Atchison, *Shaping the Next Generation* (Nashville: LifeWay Press, 1998).

Robert Crosby and Pamela Crosby, *Fun Conversation Starters for Parents and Kids* (Honor Books, March 1999).

James Dobson, *Preparing for Adolescence* (Ventura, Calif.: Regal Books, 1989).

Phil Downer, *A Father's Reward, Raising Your Children to Walk in Truth* (Eugene, Ore.: Harvest House Publishers, 1998).

Phil Downer, *Eternal Impact, Investing in the Lives of Men* (Eugene, Ore.: Harvest House Publishing, 1997).

Howard Hendricks and William Hendricks, *As Iron Sharpens Iron: Building Character in a Mentoring Relationship* (Chicago: Moody Press, 1995).

Howard Hendricks, *Heaven Help the Home* (Wheaton, Ill.: Victor Books, 1990).

David Kopp and Heather Kopp, *Praying the Bible for Your Children* (Colorado Springs: Waterbook Press, 1997).

John C. Maxwell, *Breakthrough Parenting* (Colorado Springs: Focus on the Family, 1996).

Adrian Rogers, *Ten Secrets for a Successful Family* (Wheaton, Ill.: Crossway Books, 1996).

Jim Weidmen, Kurt Bruner, Mike Nappa & Amy Nappa, *Heritage Builders: Family Night Tool Chest* (Colorado Springs: Victor, 1997).

Student Leadership University 1 (888) 260-2900, www.studentleadership.net

Chapter 4

Out of the House, Into the World

They call him 'Duck,' because he seems to like sleeping out in the rain. With no home, and living on the coast of South Florida, Duck has ample opportunity to live up to his name. Maybe he does not mind the rain—at least it is some semblance of a bath—or maybe he is ashamed to live in the street but acts the opposite to protect his pride.

Every few days Gerald and Patsy see Duck—on a street corner, near the park, or just walking down the street like he has somewhere to go. Moved by his ready smile and saddened by his conditions, the vibrant retirees decide to become active in Duck's life. Soon, they are stopping to offer Duck a sandwich or a bowl of soup Patsy has made and put in a disposable container. At first they simply pass the food out the window, say a quick word, and go on. No point in risking anything. You never know about those kinds of people, they figure. But soon, Gerald gets more daring. He stops and talks to Duck and finds him knowledgeable. He knows the sea, having been in the Navy for 12 years, he says. One day Gerald asks Duck, "Do you know Jesus?" Duck says, "Sure, Jesus feeds me!"

Healthy families spend quantity and quality time around God's purposes

You see, the Lutheran church feeds the homeless lunch on Mondays, the Catholics feed them on Tuesdays, the Methodists on Wednesdays . . .

Gerald realizes that Duck's entire concept of Jesus is a food handout. "That's not enough," Gerald tells Patsy. "What are you going to do?" Patsy asks. For the next few weeks, Patsy eats dinner while Gerald waits. Then Patsy packages a meal for Gerald and Duck, and takes Gerald to the park, where Duck is waiting. They eat together. Every night, Gerald comes home laughing with a 'Duck story,' which are pretty much like fish stories. Gerald is anxious to tell Duck a true story, and maybe Gerald is developing trust so Duck will listen about how Jesus can change his life now and in eternity.

One night, Gerald senses it is time. After they have eaten, Gerald says, "You know, Duck, I know this food Patsy makes for us is not enough."

Duck looks surprised. "Suits me, just fine, Mr. Gerald. Miss Patsy's a fine cook!" "Oh, she is!" Gerald replies.

Gerald says, "But I'm talking about a different kind of food." Duck looks puzzled. Gerald continues, "Duck, the Bible tells me that man cannot live by bread alone."

Gerald shares the gospel. Duck melts in a heap of hurt turning to hope. He receives Christ. A long road is still ahead: vocational rehabilitation, some counseling, lessons in life skills. Gerald and Patsy walk him through it, and almost a year later Duck has a studio apartment and a steady job. Early one evening, before dinnertime, there is a knock on Gerald and Patsy's door. They open it to find Duck, far better looking than when they first met him, loaded down with bags. "Hungry?" Duck says, "I made dinner . . ."

Healthy families spend quantity and quality time around God's purposes. If we truly want our children to accept the gospel, then our commitment to Christ must spill over to those around us who do not know Christ. As families, we must make it a priority to share the good news. A major one of the best and nonthreatening ways of doing that is called ministry evangelism.

Ministry evangelism was a priority to Jesus. It should be a priority in any family that wants to live the Great Commission. The Bible tells of Jesus' compassion in many places, but none more poignantly than in Matthew 25:31-36. This is the story of the separating of the sheep and the goats.

In verses 34-36 (NKJV) Jesus says, "Come, you blessed of My Father, inherit the kingdom prepared for you from the foundation of the world: for I was hungry and you gave Me food; I was thirsty and you gave Me drink; I was a stranger and you took Me in; I was naked and you clothed Me; I was sick and you visited Me; I was in prison and you came to Me."

Asked when this occurred, Jesus answered in verse 40 (NKJV), "Inasmuch as you did it to one of the least of these My brethren, you did it to Me." In this passage, Jesus in essence says, "In the world around you, who did you see that had a need? What was the need? Did you attempt to meet it? If so, you did it for Me. If not, you failed Me."

When Jesus walked on the earth, people were drawn to Him because of His love, warmth, compassion, and mercy. Today, they will be drawn to Him, through you, the same way. Ministry evangelism was Jesus' idea. He practiced it. And as John 20:21 (NKJV) tells us, "As the Father has sent Me, I also send you." According to Charles Roesel and Don Atkinson in the book *Meeting Needs/Sharing Christ,* ministry evangelism is "caring for persons in the name of Jesus Christ. It is meeting persons at the point of their need and ministering to them physically and spiritually.

"The intent of ministry evangelism is to present the good news of God's love in order to introduce persons to Jesus," Atkinson writes. "Ministry evangelism is not manipulative. Ministry is given lovingly and unconditionally. But the reason for it all, God's love for lost persons, is always shared."[39]

Ministry evangelism requires adherence to the foundational principle set forth by Henry Blackaby in *Experiencing God*: Find out what God is doing and join Him.

Writes Atkinson: "This insight is the key to ministry evangelism. God is deeply concerned with persons who hurt. He loves them, and He wants to reconcile them to Himself. His concern, as we have seen from Scripture, is for whole persons—body, mind, and spirit. If we want to discover what God is doing, we need only look at the witness of Scripture, especially Jesus' ministry. Ministry evangelism is getting on God's agenda. It means joining Him in the work He is doing in the world and in every community."[40]

This does not mean that every person or family you and your family minister to has to be "deeply hurting" or have some obvious, profound, unmet need. It does mean you must be sensitive and aware.

It is important in this day and age to give visual evidence that Christian families are different. Christianity is something that you live and that people should want, not a list of do's and don'ts.

Your family can live its faith in full view of your friends, neighbors, and acquaintances. You can be Jesus to them. You can be on mission for God, meeting needs for the purpose of intentionally sharing the gospel.

Key Principles for Ministry Evangelism

Look—Keep your eyes open. Do you see a neighbor who seems depressed? Do you see a mother struggling to care for her children? Do you see the man next door trying to drag his new refrigerator from the pick-up to the kitchen alone? Big need or small need, you can share the love of Christ.

Listen—What are people saying and how are they saying it? Are you hearing them or only listening to the words? While they may not always be as clear as we would like, careful attention to what people say will reveal much about their needs. Pay attention.

Your family can live its faith in full view of your friends, neighbors, and acquaintances

Linger—This does not mean overstay your welcome, but it does mean to be there for your neighbors, family, and acquaintances. Invest some time. Hang over the fence talking a few minutes longer than you normally might. Stop, check in, and look and listen for how Jesus may use you to bless and ultimately to share Christ with those in your community.

Ministry evangelism is so effective, in part, because it breaks down barriers. Your intent is to share the love of Jesus and, ultimately, to share how the person you are ministering to can know Jesus Christ as their Savior. But rather than enter into dialogue on this issue by means of a theological confrontation, you are entering a relationship that breaks down barriers and builds trust. Research shows that people are more than twice as likely to allow a person to share his or her faith when evangelism is combined with simple acts of kindness.

Servanthood evangelism is a sister to ministry evangelism. Ministry evangelism calls for a longer-term involvement including the potential to build a relationship. Servanthood evangelism is most often a one-time effort, though it has proven to be very fruitful. Servanthood evangelism is a combination of simple acts of kindness and intentional personal evangelism. It can include having a free car wash just to create the opportunity to explain that you are doing it to show the love of Jesus. Door-to-door light bulb giveaways, lawn work . . . there are many service things you can do for free to help break down barriers.

The greatest opening you can get to give your testimony is to be asked, "Why do you do this?"

Below are many ideas for ministry evangelism that will help keep you on mission for Christ. Please note, this is not an exhaustive list, rather a place to start. Some of these ideas will be a perfect match for your personality, giftedness, and situation, while others will not. These should trigger your own ideas based on the needs around you. The ideas are arranged according to the Concentric Circles of Concern developed by Oscar Thompson.

Concentric Circles is based on the concept of building relationships for lifestyle evangelism as a Christian moves from self to others.

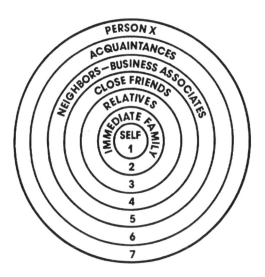

The seven circles are 1) self, 2) immediate family, 3) relatives, 4) close friends, 5) business associates and neighbors, 6) acquaintances, and 7) person X.

Wrote Thompson, "With Person X, our life-styles do not have to be consistent. We can talk and then be on our way. There is nothing wrong with telling Person X about Jesus. We are supposed to do that. God will bring these people into our lives; but if we cannot tell people in Circles 2 through 6 about the Lord, we are hypocritical. We are play acting. We are unreal people. If we are genuine, we will want to share with those closest to us."[41]

Tips for Effective Family Evangelism

Make Sure Your Family Unit is Truly a "Family Unit"

Phil Downer says, "If you want to have trouble, just try doing family ministry without strong relationships within the family."[42] Too often, fathers are involved in men's Bible study, mothers in women's Bible study, and children in youth groups. There is nothing wrong with any of those things, but if each family member is on a totally separate spiritual track, the family will not work well together. This is why family devotions and specific ministry actions are so important. They keep the family moving in the same direction. Teamwork must develop. When the spiritual environment allows for teamwork, Downer says, "Getting involved in ministry is the greatest team-building exercise for Christians that there is. We must get the family on the front lines of battle—that is where we are best. We're a fighting unit left behind by the Lord, but too often we're sitting on the pew complaining about the color of the pew pads."[43]

Your Own Needs Must Be Lower Priority

If a person is going to discover the needs of someone else, they must make that a priority. If they make someone else's needs a priority, their's must become lower. We cannot see the needs of others if we are looking at our own needs. We have to be servants. Remember the words of Jesus in John 12:24-26 (NKJV): "Unless a grain of wheat falls into the ground and dies, it remains alone; but if it dies, it produces much grain. He who loves his life will lose it, and he who hates his life in this world will keep it for eternal life. If anyone serves Me, let him follow Me; and where I am, there My servant will be also. If anyone serves Me, him My Father will honor." Remember that in the next chapter, Jesus, Who is greater, washes the feet of the disciples, who are lesser, then says, "For I have given you an example, that you should do as I have done to you" (John 13:15, NKJV).

Jesus' concept of servanthood includes responding in love when a neighbor wrongs you. It means being inconvenienced. It means doing whatever Jesus would do.

Start Now

There is a "safe period" of two to three weeks to be friendly after a new neighbor moves it. After that, it becomes more difficult to develop the relationship. What if you have already waited months or years? Try the bottom-line, honest approach. Walk over and say, "I'm a little embarrassed. We've been neighbors for three years, and we've never really talked. We'd like to have you guys over for a barbecue."

Be Patient

It takes time to build relationships. You may have some immediate success in reaching others for Christ, but there will always be relationships and circumstances that call for great patience. Is it worth it to invest years in a relationship to see someone come to Christ? We can be thankful that Christ is patient with us.

Evangelism Ideas[44]

You might be thinking, "I understand what ministry evangelism is and why it is important but, what do I do next?" In the following pages, you will find some ministry evangelism ideas along with some real life stories of how God is using His people to make a difference. This is not an exhaustive list—it is only a place to start. You will come up with many ideas of your own—ones that fit your lifestyle and circumstances. Use the ones that work, forget those that do not. But please, start building relational bridges with lost, hurting people.

For ideas on ministering to those in your immediate family (circle 2 of the Concentric Circles) refer to Chapter Three of this book.

Ideas for relatives (Circle 3)

a. Regularly invite relatives to your home for meals. When they are there, be intentional in sharing testimonies of how the Lord is working in your lives.

b. At holiday seasons, invite relatives to your home for a meal, then plan a brief devotional service relating to the holiday, but focusing on Christ.

c. Write regular notes of encouragement to your relatives, include Scripture and a reminder that you are praying for them.

d. Send "Family Update" letters annually or twice a year to your extended family. Use this vehicle to report family news, share testimonies, and very clearly share what Christ means to your family, and how others can receive Christ.

Ideas for close friends (Circle 4)

a. Invite your friend to join you for a ball game, a round of golf, a movie, and so on. You may open the conversation by saying, "I owe you an apology, I have known you a long time and I have never made time to share with you the most important part of my life." Then share your testimony and the gospel.

b. When your close friend has a need, serve him or her. Help your friend move, build a fence, take care of his or her children, or be there for that person whenever there is a need. During the break times, share your faith in Christ.

c. Invite your friend to lunch or dinner. During the conversation, bring up spiritual things. Share the gospel as God opens the door.

Ideas for business associates and neighbors (Circle 5)

a. Write a letter to your mail carrier. Your mail carrier probably knows your name and your house, but does this person know you? Does your mail carrier know you are a Christian and that you go to a local church? Does your mail carrier know you appreciate him or her delivering your mail every day? Make sure everyone in your family helps write the letter.

b. Lead your family to write a letter to your neighbors. Sure they know you, but do they know you go to church? Do they know you are Christians? Do they know you are interested when they need support and are facing family crises such as illness? Let them know your heart. Tell them you are praying for them, and do. Let them know you care.

c. Make it a point to know your neighbors' birthdays. Send them cards or make a small cake for them. If this is not possible, do something else special for them.

d. Once a month or every few months, host a game day for all the children living in your neighborhood. Plan a couple of hours of fun, games, and refreshments. At the close, lead a children's devotional, Bible study, and prayer time. Invite each child to go to church with you. Make sure you get the parents' approval for those interested.

e. Have your family host a children's craft time three to four times a year. Invite children from around the neighborhood to share in a time of making crafts. This is especially effective at the holiday season.

f. If senior adults live in your neighborhood, adopt them as grandparents. Help them with yard work. Visit them regularly as a family. Have your children create a drawing, painting, or some other type of artwork and present it to them. Help celebrate birthdays and other special events in their lives. Call or visit them regularly to check on their well being.

g. If single parents live in your neighborhood, adopt a single-parent family. Offer occasional child care so that the parent can run errands or have some time alone. Plan outings every month or so with the family. Invite them to church, and offer your family's help in times of personal challenges.

h. Organize a parents' day or night out three to four times a year. These give parents a place to leave their children while they spend some time together.

i. When you hear about a family who has faced a crisis, lead your family to pray for them, visit them briefly, or write a note of encouragement that lets the family know you are praying for them.

j. When a neighbor is ill, have your family create and deliver a homemade get well card.

k. When a family has a relative who has passed away or is in the hospital, have your family prepare and deliver a meal to them.

l. When a family has a baby, prepare a meal (ask about diet limitations in advance), and deliver it. Perhaps offer to run errands or do anything that may help in the first weeks of recovery and adjustment.

m. Every month or three to four times a year, invite a family from your neighborhood to participate in a family fellowship meal. Include not only those families you know, but also those families you do not know. It is a great opportunity to get to know families who have recently moved into your community.

n. Lead your family to conduct a Backyard Bible Club during the summer for neighborhood children. A Backyard Bible Club can be held weekly or daily for an entire week. (Materials are available at your local Christian bookstore). Perhaps your church will provide the materials.

o. Conduct a family cookout at your house. Ask those you invite to bring a dish. Consider planning a community worship service with special music, brief devotion, and perhaps a testimony by somebody in your family about how Christ has changed his or her life.

p. When your neighbors leave town on vacation or for some other reason, do their yard work while they are away. (You might want to ask in advance, in case they planned to make other arrangements such as paying for it to be done). When they return, leave a note on their door: "Welcome home! Thanks for being a good neighbor."

q. Plan a neighborhood progressive Christmas dinner.
r. Host a baby shower for a neighbor who is expecting.
s. Deliver freshly baked cookies or other goodies to a family who has recently moved into your neighborhood.
t. Invite a family who has recently moved into your neighborhood to your home for dessert.

Tony is struggling up the stairs with boxes of books. He has already managed to do what appeared at first impossible—get his chest of drawers into his new apartment. Exhausted, sweating, and favoring a jammed finger, Tony is fully aware of the first drawback to moving to a town where he knows no one—no help moving in.

"Neighbors" walk by regularly. They are not the friendliest bunch. Most do not make eye contact. "Probably afraid I'll ask them to help move a piano!" Tony thinks. Hours later, Tony is finally through. He makes a mental note: "If I ever see anyone in this situation, I'm lending a hand!"

About two months later, he gets his chance. As he arrives home on Friday evening, he sees a mid-sized moving truck backed up to the apartment building next to his. Tony lingers in the car after parking, trying to see who it is. A single young man is shuttling things back and forth. Tony goes inside quickly, puts on some old jeans and a jersey, and goes over to help. "Hi, I'm Tony," he says, extending his hand to the man as he comes out of the apartment. "Hi, my name's Chuck. Good to meet you." "By yourself?" Tony asks. "Yeah, I'm afraid so." "Well, I'm free. How about I give you hand?" Tony asks. "Great! I'll buy the beer later," Chuck says. "That won't be necessary," Tony says, smiling inside, as he grabs a box. "I was wondering if anybody was ever going to offer to help," Chuck says. Tony laughed to himself again. He resisted the temptation to say, "Believe me, buddy, they weren't."

Tony and Chuck live in the same complex for three years, and gradually Tony gains Chuck's trust and friendship, though they are very different: Tony is focused, mature, devout in his faith. Chuck is a party animal and womanizer who left his wife and daughter before moving to Tony's town. But Tony works at the relationship with one goal in mind, and two years after moving from that complex—having maintained the friendship—he leads Chuck to Jesus Christ.

u. Plant a vegetable garden and regularly share the harvest with neighbors, cultivating relationships with them.

v. Plan and promote a Halloween-alternative party—a harvest festival—with food, games, and a devotional and testimony time.

w. When a new family moves into the neighborhood, take them dessert, bread, or some other treat as a way to begin a relationship.

x. Allow your children to plan regular Saturday night sleepovers for neighborhood children and—in advance—invite the children to go to church with you. Offer to take them in future weeks, if the parents agree.

y. Be conscious of latchkey children in the neighborhood, and offer to watch them, whether it is each day or a certain day of the week.

z. Organize a car pool for working parents.

aa. At Christmas, bake bread or cookies, wrap a JESUS video in Christmas paper, then present both of these as a gift to a lost neighbor.

bb. Plan a neighborhood-watch block party. Most of the people in the area are interested in safety. Invite local police to give safety tips, then have people share briefly who they are and their interest. This will give an opportunity to develop relationships and also for you to share your interest in spiritual things.

cc. At Christmas, plan a ministry to people in institutions such as a local prison or youth who are in a local rehabilitation hospital.

It is the Christmas season, and Ben and Margaret's children want to do something special. "How about a birthday party for Jesus!" Margaret suggests to Katelyn (9), Jason (7), and Ricky (4). Everyone agrees it is a great idea. Invitations are made, and for two afternoons, Margaret and the children walk through the neighborhood delivering them to 20 neighbors. Margaret is careful to tell the neighbors, "We're going to tell the Christmas story—how Jesus came to Earth as a tiny baby—and why that's important." That way, no parent is surprised by what the children are taught. The parents are encouraged to attend, too.

About a week before Christmas, it is time for the party. Jesus has a birthday cake. There are party hats and all the typical birthday trim. About halfway through the celebration, Ben takes a few minutes to read the Christmas story from the Bible. Then he says, "This is a very important story for our family, because we believe Jesus Christ was sent to the world to save us from our sins. We live according to the Bible. We follow Jesus. Moms and Dads, we hope this is something you'll learn more about, and we'll be glad to talk to you about it, if you want."

No pressure. No complex theology. Just fun, Jesus, and the opportunity to share. Several children begin attending church with Ben and Margaret's family. Soon, some parents begin attending, too. Ben, Margaret, Katelyn, Jason, and Ricky have developed the relationships that could lead many people to have a glorious reason for celebrating Jesus' birthday.

Ideas for acquaintances (Circle 6)

a. Serve soft drinks or ice water to the people who pick up your trash. If they come when you are not at home, make sure the drinks are marked clearly so they will know the drinks are for them. People very seldom show any kindness to trash collectors. Canned drinks or refreshments in disposable cups allow them to drink on the run and are greatly appreciated.

b. Distribute copies of the New Testament to the people who deliver your mail, pick up your trash, and perform other services for your family.

c. Give a handwritten invitation to your mail carrier, trash collectors, cashiers, and so on, when your church has special programs such as musicals, Vacation Bible School, or Christmas and Easter programs.

d. At Christmas, Easter, and other holidays, plan and promote a special fellowship for your mail carrier, trash collectors, other community servants, and their families. Make it a special time of food and fellowship in a Christian atmosphere. Consider planning a brief worship time with the music presented by your family or a special guest. Include a brief devotional, such as a reading of the Christmas story or the account of the resurrection during Easter.

e. Join with other Christian families from your church or neighborhood to prepare a fellowship for fire fighters or police officers in your community. Work with these special people to schedule a convenient date and time. The holiday season is an especially good time to show your appreciation. Consider planning a brief worship service, including music from family members or guests.

f. Encourage your children to set up a free refreshment stand in the neighborhood. If the children are able, have them explain, when asked why it is free, that they are doing this to show the love of Jesus. Parents will want to be nearby to share with adults. Witnessing booklets, suitable for children, can be made available.

g. Adopt an international student.

The previous owners of Randy Reynolds' new home have left mounds of junk in the garage. Distressed at the clean up required, Randy asks a neighbor about garbage pick-up. "If you'll put it by the street Friday morning, they'll get it," the neighbor says. "But it's so much—you might want to be out there to help them."

Thursday night Randy spends an hour hauling the mess—old car parts, toys . . . you name it—to the curb. First thing Friday he is up and waiting. The garbage truck arrives at 7:30 a.m., and four African-American men starting loading the junk. Randy helps, all the while mindful that he has so many other things to do. He quickly thanks the men and says, "Anything I can do for you?" He did not mean it. In fact, he almost instantly regrets asking, as one of the men says, "Yeah, how about something to drink." Randy trudges to the house, thinking about all the time he is wasting. He grabs a six-pack of soft drinks and takes it back to the men. As each of the men takes one, one steps right up to Randy's face and says, "In all my 13 years in sanitation, you're the only person, white or black, who has ever asked if he could ever do something for me."

Randy drowns in conviction, but he allows the Lord to use that conviction for His purpose. Then and there Randy commits to being a minister to his community, to being a witness for Christ "as he goes" and everywhere he goes.

Every Friday morning since that day 13 years ago, as many as three garbage trucks will pull up in front of Randy's home. Randy (and usually his children) is out there with refreshments and an encouraging word. The effort of Randy and his family has led to many opportunities to share Christ and minister.

Ideas for Person X (Circle 7)

a. Prior to vacation, lead your family in making gift bags filled with candy. Share these gifts with waiters/waitresses, housekeepers, and others that serve your family while on vacation.

b. Have your family adopt a local nursing home. Plan regular visits and get to know the residents.

c. If your family sings or has other musical talents, perform for residents in health care facilities.

d. During the Christmas season, go caroling in a health care facility.

e. Contact the chaplain of a local jail or prison and inquire about an angel tree ministry. This is a special ministry conducted during the Christmas season. Names of families of incarcerated individuals are written on slips of paper and placed on a Christmas tree. The church families select a family from this tree and provide Christmas gifts for family members.

f. Lead your family in planning and promoting a children's game day in an inner-city housing project. Contact the housing project management and tell them you would like to provide children's programming at no charge. After playing children's games, serve light refreshments, share a Bible story, have prayer time, and have someone give a testimony.

g. Create your own family fix-it squad for Christ. Contact your Department of Human Services and ask for a list of families who need some home repairs done. Then go and do fix-up or painting projects.

h. Adopt a refugee family. Contact your denominational headquarters or your local government and ask about refugee resettlement. Adopt a family, perhaps helping with clothing, food, and furniture, for example. Cultivate them into God's family.

i. Plant a vegetable garden and regularly share the harvest with people in homeless shelters, sharing about Jesus as the source of provision, cultivating relationships with them as you do.

Family Evangelism with Special-Needs Children

Individuals with special needs and their families represent one of the largest unreached people groups in America. Thus, it is imperative that local congregations catch the vision to reach this group with the gospel. According to special education teachers and those fluent in this kind of ministry, the most effective approach is family to family contact through genuine concern and servant-oriented ministries.

Sadly, there are several misconceptions relating to special-needs children. First, most people tend to lump all impairments into the same category with the assumption that physical needs are always related to mental deficiency. Nothing could be further from the truth. Like everyone else, special-needs children and adults must be dealt with individually. The truth is those with physical or mental challenges need the saving grace of the gospel message. In many cases, these individuals will excel beyond their supposed difficulties and often become bold, personal witnesses.

This leads to the second misconception that somehow special-needs individuals must always have limitations placed upon their activities and behavior. This is a wrong assumption. If you are the Christian parent of a special-needs child, please know that, like all other Christians, those with impairments must also be obedient to the call of evangelism. This means that families of special-needs children must not

Individuals with special needs and their families represent one of the largest unreached people groups in America

limit their community involvement in evangelism for the "sake" of the child or the parent. In most cases, special-needs individuals can be very effective in evangelism and often become an asset in doing family to family ministries.

Suppose there is a family dealing with a special-needs situation in your community. Who could be better prepared to minister to this family evangelistically? You already understand many of the difficulties and challenges. It only takes a sacrifice of time, a strong trust in God, genuine concern, and a willingness to listen and get involved in kingdom business. In the end, this will build family togetherness, create memories, and develop a greater confidence among both the physically and mentally challenged, as well as the family members involved.

For instance, one family of a child with cerebral palsy spoke of how they participated in door-to-door servant evangelism projects by allowing their excited young girl to be the first person met at the door bearing gifts. In one case it was fudge at Christmas, in another instance it was batteries for smoke detectors, or bags of microwave popcorn with a card attached stating, "pop in and visit our church sometime." Those visited were introduced to each participant, given a special gift by a "special" child, then told that "Christ loved them." In some of the cases they prayed with individuals; in others, they were able to share the gospel. In every instance, the participants learned the same important lesson about fulfilling the Great Commission, regardless of physical or mental limitations. Both the young girl and those visited received an extraordinary blessing.

As far as ministering family to family with a special-needs situation, consider several options like providing "parents' night out" opportunities, especially where the needs are chronic and demand around-the-clock care. This may even demand the securing of a nurse who is trained to administer proper care. In some situations you may only require a mild dose of patience and a special ability to administer the love of Christ. Ask the Lord to show you how to proceed. You might also consider preparing meals or providing some new clothes. If they are a good quality, consider offering some of the slightly used clothes that your children have outgrown. Most of all, be genuine and build relationships.

Do not give up, even if the special-needs family does not respond immediately. Remember, above all people, they know the difference between loving concern and pity. These individuals do not need pity. On the contrary, they need Jesus and the affirmation of dignity and self-worth that is inherent to the gospel. Love them family to family.

Again, these ideas are a place to start. Use the ones that fit your personality and situation. Come up with your own creative ministry ideas. Remember this, you reach those hard to reach family members, close friends, and neighbors through serving them. Healthy families will find fun, practical—as well as creative—ways to minister. It is all part of spending quality, quantity, and purposeful time while passing the baton of faith to the next generation.

Through ministry and acts of kindness, relational bridges are built over which the gospel can be shared. Remember, Jesus came to seek and to save that which was lost (see Luke 19:10). He came to meet their physical and spiritual needs. After you meet their physical and emotional needs through ministry, allow God to use you to meet their spiritual needs by verbalizing the gospel. You might be thinking, "I don't have the gift" or "I can't do that." In Chapter 6, you will learn how to cross relational bridges through sharing your faith in Christ in a nonthreatening way.

Steps to Making it Yours

Family Readiness Questions

There is a time for everything. You began by reading the book. Now to help gather your thoughts, review what you have read by answering the Family Readiness Questions.

1. One of the best ways to share the good news is through _____ evangelism.

2. People were drawn to Jesus (and still are today through us) because of His _____, _____, _____, and _____.

3. What are the three guiding principles for ministry evangelism? How can your family be involved in your community in each of the principles?

    1.

    2.

    3.

4. What is the difference between ministry evangelism and servanthood evangelism?_____

5. What are the seven concentric circles?

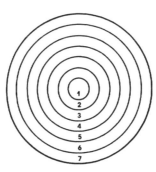

Family Applications

The second step in studying Family to Family *is to discover adjustments through prayers. To help you identify areas in which God may be speaking to you, work through the Family Applications. At the end of each, ask God to reveal any adjustments He wants you to make.*

1. Talk about ways each family member shows love, warmth, compassion, and mercy with one another and among friends.

2. To help bring cohesion to your family, list all of the activities each family member is involved in at church. Next, try to tie those activities together (i.e., what do they have in common?). Finally, consider getting involved in a single spiritual activity as a family once a quarter.

3. Give each family member a different color marker or crayon. Next, read through the list of evangelism ideas described in this chapter. Have each family member mark ideas that appeal to him or her.

4. How can each family member make others' needs a priority over his or her own (see Phil. 4:13)?

5. Review the concentric circles illustration described in this chapter. Name people in circles three through six and begin praying for an opportunity to minister to and share the gospel with them.

Family Building Activities

The activities allow your family to experience the results of the adjustments you are making. As you select several and carry them out, talk about what God is doing in the life of your family. These activities are not an end unto themselves; they create a teachable moment.

1. Choose one activity for each circle (or develop your own) and plan how you will implement them over the next six months. Involve everyone in the family and make sure the activities are consistent with your family mission statement.

2. Plan a meal with some neighbors you know are hurting. Look for opportunities to share the gospel.

Scripture

The following verses were found in the fourth chapter of Family to Family. *For further application you could allow each family member to choose the verse or passage that meant the most to them and allow them to tell why.*

Matthew 25:31-36
John 20:21

Additional Resources:

Donald A. Atkinson and Charles L. Roesel, *Meeting Needs, Sharing Christ* (Nashville: LifeWay Press, 1995).

Alvin L. Reid and David A. Wheeler, *Servanthood Evangelism,* (Alpharetta, Ga.: North American Mission Board, 1999).

Chapter 5

Out of Your World, Into Your Church

It has been six months since the McMichaels claimed their street for Christ. In prayer, they dedicated themselves to trying to share the gospel with someone in each of the 17 houses on Oakmont Trail. Two or three times a week, they walk up and down the street, silently praying for the members of each household, asking the Lord to make their neighbors sensitive to the gospel and themselves sensitive to their neighbors.

Opportunities to share come quickly in some places. The Browns, Coombs, and McDonalds are easy to get to know. The Warrens seem suspicious every time they are spoken to. The McMichaels remain patient and sensitive to opportunities: Dad helps the man down the street chop down a dead tree; Vicki, 17, offers to baby-sit on the spur of the moment when she learns a neighbor is in a bind. Occasionally when family members are asked why they are helping, and they give their standard, but sincere answer, offered with a smile: "Just trying to show God's love in a practical way!"

You minister in the neighborhood. You minister in and through the church. But shouldn't the two be linked?

"I see that we're building relationships and making progress," Dad said one night at the dinner table. "But . . . I don't know. We need something to pull it together. Anybody know what I mean?" It was quiet for a minute then Mom spoke up. "I get the same feeling. Jenique told me about something Pastor Stan has been teaching on Sunday nights in a class on evangelism strategies. He's been talking about the church sponsoring block parties. You know, putting on an event for the neighborhood, sponsored by the church, but not at church."

"Cool," 12-year-old Benjamin says. "It's almost the end of the school year; how about we celebrate that? We could have a killer neighborhood softball game."

"Good idea, Benjamin," Dad chimes in, his eyes brightening as the wheels turn. "But . . . that may take some planning. How about we think about it for July 4, you know, so we have time to do it right?"

"That'll work," Vickie says. "We can rent the clubhouse by the pool, have a big get-together, and get Pastor Stan to come and speak and invite everybody to church! Is that how Jenique says it works, Mom?"

"That sounds about right," Mom says. "But we know how to find out. Let's get on it."

You minister in the neighborhood. You minister in and through the church. But shouldn't the two be linked? Absolutely. There are many easy ways to do it. If you are going to be a healthy, on-mission family, you will want to show those to whom you minister a place where they can fellowship with Christians and mature in Christ—that is the church.

The McMichaels made a wise move, and there are others. Integrating your family's ministry with the church is crucial. Neighborhood block parties, family mission trips, and the JESUS Video Project are among the most effective ways to bridge to the church.

Neighborhood Block Parties

Whether in a rich, poor, or middle-class neighborhood, the evangelistic block party can be very effective. Success stories abound of even small churches drawing several hundred to a block party. Larger churches have drawn thousands.

An evangelistic block party involves identifying a neighborhood and providing a meal and program. Activities that suit the people in the neighborhood and the facilities are arranged, with special activities for children. Music is a vital part. A testimony or gospel message should be provided.

In the case of the McMichaels, the idea was for the church to sponsor the event in the McMichaels' neighborhood, drawing on the McMichaels' relationships, thus bridging the church to the community.

The evangelistic block party should be:

> *Inclusive*—As you meet your neighbors you will doubtless meet other evangelical believers. Include them. Work together to impact your neighborhood or subdivision.

Intimate—It is a special evangelism event using a personal evangelism thrust, thus making guests feel they are the center of attention.

Intentional—Evangelism should be the priority, and proper planning will have the party flow to the point of a gospel presentation. An interesting program, food, and entertainment are among the vehicles that carry the event to the point of sharing the message.

> **People will come to an event of this type who would never come to church**

Informal—Yes, you must do a lot of planning, but it is, in effect, "planned relaxation" or "planned fun." Have a structure, but do not be ruled by it. Reaching people is the point, so the focus of the hosts (who may be very numerous) must be directed toward the people.

Interesting—Make the program relevant and fun. If there is a message or a testimony, keep it (or them) short and crisp. Plan activities according to the interests and make-up of the neighborhood.

Imaginative—Be creative. Many holidays, events, interests, and seasons can be a good excuse to have a party. It may be a Super Bowl party, a fall festival, a pasta party, an end-of-the-school-year party . . . think, be creative. The only firm rules are: Show Christ's love and share the gospel.[45]

People will come to an event of this type who would never come to church. Once people have met others from the church, they may feel more open to attend. Attendance at a neighborhood block party gives the church an open door for continued ministry, evangelism, and follow-up.

Family Mission Trips

Dawn has seen the empty eyes and hollow faces of death row inmates. She has seen the utter squalor on the streets of Brazil. Inner-city decay in the United States is not foreign to Dawn's eyes, either.

None of these are pretty sights, but they have permanently touched the 18-year-old heart. Many in the above settings have been eternally transformed by the message brought through her and others with whom she was on mission.

Dawn Jenkins' way of life has been to minister to others; her family has always been on mission for God. Mission trips to Brazil and countless national and local trips, including singing for death row inmates, offer a rich background of experience from which to say, "It changed my attitude and how I view life. I've look at people around me and seen how much God has given me."

Do all of those trips get boring? "No!" Dawn says. "It's a different experience every time you go, and to see all those people come to Christ is amazing. That never gets boring!" Dawn's team saw 300 come to Christ on the first international trip she took, 42 the first time she shared her faith.

"I always feel awkward at first, but God gives you the words to say. He'll help you through it." Dawn's father, Wayne, says, "She's rubbed shoulders with the kinds of people that in most settings we say, 'stay away from.' She has learned, as we all must, that everyone needs Jesus, and there is a way to reach any kind of people."

Your family cannot only reach its neighborhood, but it can reach beyond it to the city, state, and world through family mission trips. These can be done independently or in partnership with your church, association, or other ministry agencies for family mission trips.

Some benefits of family mission trips:

- **It gives your family a sense of purpose**.
- **It is shared ministry. The Jenkins mentioned above have passed down the tradition.** Two grown daughters have taken their husbands on trips. In each home, space is dedicated to memorabilia from the many trips. There is a clearly identifiable heritage of ministry that runs through the extended family.
- **It models evangelism to the children.**
- **It equips your family to share the gospel—anywhere, not just on the trip.**

- It instills in your family appreciation for the things you have, as well as appreciation of other cultures.
- It instills in your family a "Christian world view," that is, a view that more accurately reflects Christ's view of the world.

The following are keys to preparing for a family mission trip:

- **Begin with commitment.**
- **Make a plan and follow through.** Start with one trip, whether a local trip to the jail or prison, or an international mission trip. If possible, plan to make return trips. Instill in the family a lifestyle of witnessing "as you go." This will teach your family to be on mission for Christ.
- **Plan for spending time and money.** This will take some sacrifice, but if the Lord is in it, and you work diligently, He will provide. Many families take a week of vacation for their mission trip, but they consider it no loss because of the benefits gained. Fund-raising, if necessary, will likely have to begin well in advance. Careful planning will be honored.
- **Equip your family.** Do not set your family up for frustration by failing to clearly educate them on where you are going, and what you will be doing. Then train them how to do it. There are many resources, written and seminars, available through bookstores, Christian agencies, and so on.
- **Stress personal preparation.** This means be ready spiritually and physically. Though you should always be spending time with Jesus, spend more time in specific spiritual preparation for this trip. Be physically rested and prepared. Rushing into a mission trip without proper spiritual and physical preparation can lead to frustration or failure.

Many churches initiate "family" mission trips. Some start out with trips in the United States, then go overseas. Some alternate between the two. Clearview Baptist Church in Franklin, Tenn., regularly has about 32 people on a domestic mission trip. They have ranged in age from 4 to 66.

Here are three things churches must stress to families.
1. **Missions is not just for adults. It is a family experience.**
2. **Missions is fun.**
3. **Missions is rewarding.** One 4-year-old girl went with Clearview on her first mission trip. Her mother was very concerned because they were going to the inner city. One day as they were doing Vacation Bible School at the mission, the mom noticed that her daughter and a little girl of another race were arm-in-arm. That afternoon on the playground, the little girl told her mom, "This is my best friend."

If your family wants to take a family mission trip, and your church does not provide such opportunities, approach your pastor. Tell the pastor, "This will personalize missions for our church and for our family better than anything we would do, and would teach that at an early age children can be involved in missions—that it is not just a life calling to be a career missionary." Consider checking state and association ministry groups for possible mission trips you can join.

Consider giving a week of your vacation every year or at least every other year for a family mission trip. God will use your family to make an eternal difference in the lives of hurting people and in the process you will be passing the baton of your faith in Christ to your children.

The JESUS Video

The JESUS Video is a feature-length film that shares the story of Christ according to the Gospel of Luke. It has been seen by more than 1.5 billion people in more than 220 nations and translated into more than 400 languages. More than 73 million people are known to have accepted Jesus Christ after viewing it.

But it is working great in English, too! Recently, a JESUS Video was sent to every household in Alabama: 1.7 million. The response cards noting decisions for Christ are still being received. In one area of 50 homes, 48 decisions for Christ were recorded.

> *Twenty-one percent of Americans receive Christ when given a clear presentation of the gospel through the JESUS Video*

According to statistics gathered by the JESUS Video Project ministry team, "Twenty-one percent of Americans receive Christ when given a clear presentation of the gospel through the JESUS Video." In Syracuse, N.Y., recently, a salvation was recorded for every video given, based on three people watching the video.

The Center for World Missions credits the JESUS film with "touching more lives than any other evangelistic effort in human history."

The JESUS Video Project (1-800-29JESUS) can provide details on the low cost (as low as $5 per video) and easy process of distributing the JESUS Video. It can be a churchwide project, or simply the ministry of your family to your neighborhood.[46]

The JESUS Video is an effective way for nonChristians to come to Christ. It is also a nonthreatening, effective way for Christians to share with their neighbors and friends. Because the video is packaged as a gift, it is both personal evangelism (shared door-to-door) and event evangelism (watched in a group).

It is an incredibly effective way to get the gospel into your neighborhood. It creates opportunities for follow-up. In fact, you would not do it without plans to follow-up. And it is easy. It is nonthreatening to the person witnessing and to the person it is given to. You can deliver it as a gift without having to say much of anything.

Encourage your church to get involved in the JESUS Video Project. The church can use the video as a tool to saturate a particular neighborhood with the gospel. You can use it to give to neighbors and acquaintances as you go on mission for God with your family.

The healthy, on-mission family will make a conscious effort to integrate ministry and the church. The missions-minded church will make that easy for the family.

Steps to Making it Yours

Family Readiness Questions
There is a time for everything. You began by reading the book. Now to help gather your thoughts, review what you've read by answering the Family Readiness Questions.

1. Integrating your family's _____ with the _____ is crucial.

2. Three of the most effective ways to bridge your ministry with the church are:

    1. _____

    2. _____

    3. _____

3. Match the block party principle with its definition.
   A block party should be:

   a. Inclusive _____ Make guests feel they are the center of attention.

   b. Intimate _____ Make the program relevant and fun.

   c. Intentional _____ Be creative. Use any "excuse" to have a party.

   d. Informal _____ A way to work with other evangelical neighbors.

   e. Interesting _____ Evangelism should be the priority.

f. Imaginative _____ The block party should be
"planned" relaxation.

4. What is the significance of going on a family mission trip? How would this be different than each family member going on a separate trip?

5. The _____ _____ has touched more lives than any other evangelistic effort in human history.

Family Applications
The second step in studying Family to Family *is to discover adjustments through prayer. To help you identify areas in which God may be speaking to you, work through the Family Applications. At the end of each, ask God to reveal any adjustments He wants you to make.*

> **If you are going to be a healthy family, it is important that you prepare yourself to effectively communicate how a person can receive Jesus Christ as Savior**

1. Think of at least five creative reasons to host a neighborhood block party.

2. Rank, in order, the benefits of a family mission trip. Discuss the reasons you chose the top two.

3. Look at your family mission statement and discuss how taking a family mission trip would support your family's purpose.

4. If your family has already gone on a family mission trip, plan to talk to Sunday School classes in your church. Share your experiences, photos, struggles, and rewards. Use information from this chapter to supplement your talk.

5. To whom could your family give the JESUS Video? How would you present it to them? How would you follow up with them?

Family Building Activities
The activities allow your family to experience the results of the adjustments you are making. As you select several and carry them out, talk about what God is doing in the life of your family. These activities are not an end unto themselves; they create a teachable moment.

1. Begin a prayerwalk in your neighborhood.

2. Play charades with your family, acting out places your family could go on a family mission trip. Some examples include an orphanage, a prison, a resort area, a mall, and another country.

3. Dad, during the next two weeks, take each of your children out to do his or her favorite activity. On the way home, talk about ways to reach people at those places (e.g., the mall, ball game, and park).

4. Purchase the JESUS Video for everyone in your neighborhood. Make cards from you to your neighbors and distribute them. Follow up with each family over the next two months.

5. Watch the JESUS Video as a family (how about a bowl of popcorn?). Discuss the way the gospel is presented in the video.

Chapter 6

SHARING THE MESSAGE

In the expanse of the Great Smoky Mountain National Park near Cades Cove in Tennessee, volunteers and park rangers walk shoulder-to-shoulder through thick forest, battling time and great odds to find a 5-year-old boy.

He has been missing for days, having wandered away from his parents, and hope of his survival is waning fast. Helpless and defenseless, he faces cold nights and dangerous animals. He has no chance on his own of negotiating the vast forest. The little boy is separated from all life supports—parents, food, shelter, and clothing. He has no map—even if he could read it.

The above child was never found. His tale represents supreme lostness in the physical realm. In the spiritual realm, the reality is much worse.

If you are going to be a healthy family, one that lives God's commandments and fulfils the Great Commission, it is important that you prepare yourself to effectively communicate how a person can receive Jesus Christ as Savior. There are two reasons this is important. First, through the information you gleaned in the last two chapters you have learned how to build bridges through service and ministry. However, a bridge is not worth much if you do not take the next step by crossing it. If you build a relational bridge to share Christ and then do not communicate the message, then your friend goes to hell

If you are going to be a healthy family, it is important that you prepare yourself to effectively communicate how a person can receive Jesus Christ as Savior

feeling really good about his of her relationship with you. You must be very intentional about sharing "the Way, the Truth and the Life" through Jesus Christ. This chapter will provide information you can use to share Christ in a nonthreatening way. Second, sharing Jesus with others is a vital part of your passing the baton of faith in Christ to those you love most—your family.

One of the first steps in learning to communicate your faith is to understand the lostness of those you seek to reach.

Luke 19:10 (NKJV) tells us, "For the Son of Man has come to seek and to save that which was lost." The word "lost" in the Bible comes from the Greek word *apollumi*, which means, "to utterly destroy." In various places in the Bible it means "to be ruined or rendered useless, to be wasted, to perish."

Spiritually, to be lost simply means to be separated from God. We are lost because of sin. "When Adam sinned, spiritual death and separation came into the human race. A barrier of sin came between God and humans as the result of human sin," Darrell Robinson author of *The Doctrine of Salvation*, writes, referencing Romans 3:9.[47]

Romans 3:10-12 (NKJV) reports the universal ravages of sin. It is a commentary on the condition of the lost: "There is none righteous, no, not one; there is none who understands; there is none who seeks after God. They have all turned aside; they have together become unprofitable; there is none who does good, no, not one."

But lostness does not have to be neither our destiny nor the destiny of our friends, associates or neighbors. Through Jesus Christ, we have a choice. Jesus said in John 10:10 (NKJV), "The thief does not

The destiny of the lost in eternity is an unparalleled tragedy

come except to steal, and to kill, and to destroy. I have come that they may have life, and that they may have it more abundantly."

A glorious future? Or hell? Man has the choice. The consequences of lostness are simple yet profound:

1. Wasted existence of this present life.
2. Eternal separation from God in hell.

"The destiny of the lost in eternity is an unparalleled tragedy," Robinson writes.[48] That should be ample motivation to share the message of the only One who can save us from eternal damnation. The people of God must regain a passion for reaching lost people. You are a lifeline to a drowning man, a rescuing hand to those around you.

The Importance of Prayer in Evangelism

Leonard is an alcoholic, a rough man, lacking in tenderness and affection. At 71 years of age, the children are grown, raised mostly by their mother, Eleanor, even though Leonard was physically there. They have six grown children who have been divorced a combined eight times. There are two alcoholics among the group. Four of the six are struggling, having been deeply damaged in some fashion by their father's influence. The two others ran from the trouble and in so doing found Christ. Eleanor accepted Jesus, too, at 35, in a crisis over whether to kill Leonard, leave him, or surrender to Jesus.

Eleanor and Leonard are still together, thanks to the determination and faithfulness of Eleanor, who—along with their children—has prayed daily for Leonard's salvation. Is there any hope? Not on the surface. He mocks God and the church. He says Christians are weak and calls Christianity a crutch. Eleanor has lived on the edge of despair, at times doubting whether God could, or would want to, reach a man like Leonard.

Flash forward 13 years. Leonard is 84. By now his liver should have petrified and killed him, but he is vibrant, more active than at 71. He is greeting newcomers in Sunday School—something he has done for 12 years—ever since that day when, coming out of a drunken stupor, he finally looked himself in the mirror and examined his life, his wife, and his children, and his future.

Eleanor's tender words about Jesus' love came rushing back to him that day. The image of her on her knees each morning and night floods his mind and heart. He digs up numerous letters his two Christian children have written (without Eleanor knowing it, he has saved them in a box in the storage building). One of them has a little gospel booklet in it. Instead of laughing at it as he has before, he reads it. Desperation and lostness filled his soul. He sees his separation from God. Finally, he desperately calls out to God, who mercifully answers.

Eleanor cried tears of joy for days. Leonard is transformed, showing her affection he had never expressed. Leonard told Eleanor almost every day for the rest of his life: "Jesus changed me because you and the kids prayed for so long. You never gave up on me, and neither did He." What difference does prayer make? If we believe the Bible, it makes a great difference. James 5:16 (NKJV) tells us, "The effective, fervent prayer of a righteous man avails much."

You cannot be an on-mission Christian, one that carries the message, the power, the strength, and the salvation of the Father unless you are in daily communication with the "Mission Commander." If you are going to embody the element of a healthy family that calls for your significance to be found in Christ, and if you are going to mentor your children to pray, you must understand the critical importance of praying for the lost.

Prayer is commanded in Scripture. In Luke 18:1 (NKJV) we are told

> *Jesus changed me because you and the kids prayed for so long*

"men always ought to pray and not lose heart." In 1 Thessalonians 5:17 we are told to "pray without ceasing," an obvious, though not literal, expression of the priority of prayer. It indicates maintaining an attitude of prayer in all things. This attitude of prayer is crucial to our effectiveness in dialogue with those who do not know Christ.

Colossians 4:2 (NKJV) instructs us to "continue earnestly in prayer, being vigilant in it with thanksgiving." Vigilant indicates to be doggedly observant and persistent. Do you pray that way?

More than just being commanded to pray, the Word of God makes it plain that we are to pray for those who do not know Christ. In Matthew 6:9-10 (NKJV), Jesus says, "In this manner, therefore, pray: Our Father in heaven, Hallowed be Your name. Your kingdom come. Your will be done on earth as it is in heaven." Then 2 Peter 3:9 (NKJV) tells us part of the Lord's will when it says He is "not willing that any should perish but that all should come to repentance."

Because He desires all to come to repentance (and thus salvation), we must show and tell people the Way and pray diligently for them to receive Christ. Do you have a list of lost family, friends, and acquaintances that you pray for daily? You should.

Romans 10:1 (NKJV) tells us, "Brethren, my heart's desire and prayer to God for Israel is that they may be saved." Paul, the author of Romans, prayed for lost people. The implication could not be any more clearly: We must pray for lost people.

In 1 Timothy 2:1-4 (NKJV) we read, "Therefore I exhort first of all that supplications, prayers, intercessions, and giving of thanks be made for all men, for kings and all who are in authority, that we may lead a quiet and peaceable life in all godliness and reverence. For this is good and acceptable in the sight of God our Savior, who desires all men to be saved and to come to the knowledge of the truth."

If God desires all to come to a relationship with Him, we cannot help but pray for the same. Richard Leach used the acronym HEART in *Praying Your Friends to Christ* to help us remember how to pray for lost people:

H for their Heart to be receptive to the gospel
E for their spiritual Eyes and Ears to be opened
A for their Attitude toward sin to match God's Attitude
R for God to Release them to believe
T after Trusting in Christ to live a Transforming life[49]

Thom Rainer's research on churches that are reaching the lost people reveals that prayer ranks in importance with biblical preaching and teaching.

A variety of prayer methods have been effective. Prayerwalking involves a group or individual walking through a neighborhood or area and praying specifically for the people who live there. List praying is another option. Develop a list of lost neighbors, friends, family members, and associates and pray for them. A third is to begin a neighborhood house of prayer. That includes any place where one or more individuals come to pray for the salvation of lost people.

> *An on-mission Christian cannot be effective without the power of prayer*

Regardless of how you pray, be sure to pray. An on-mission Christian cannot be effective without the power of prayer. It has been well said, "You can do more than pray after you have prayed, but you cannot do more than pray until you have prayed."

You are Not Alone—The Work of the Holy Spirit in Evangelism

As Chris prays and reads the Bible, an impression overwhelms him: Be vulnerable, be sensitive to an opportunity to share Jesus. He continued the day with the feeling that something special was going to happen.

Boarding a plane for a business trip, Chris prays for the opportunity to tell someone about Jesus. He sat down next to a middle-aged couple. Casual conversation begins as the plane takes off. Soon, they ask his profession. Explaining his role in a para-church ministry, Chris says that he "tries to show people the way to Jesus Christ." The kind looks of the couple change quickly to disgust, as one says, "Why in the world would you do something like that?"

Such a response would normally cause most people to become defensive or to attack. Chris remembers the Holy Spirit's earlier prompting: Be vulnerable. Though the couple has offended him, he decides to reveal his heart.

"Well, you see, when I was 17 years of age, my brother and best friend and I were under a curse of depression," Chris says softly to the couple. "My brother and my best friend committed suicide. I found Christ."

As soon as the words leave Chris' mouth, the couple breaks down in tears. They were in route to pick up the body of their son, who had committed suicide.

Chris used the opportunity to minister deeply to this couple, Christians who had turned away from Christ. How did this happen? Let's look at the Holy Spirit's role. The Holy Spirit:

1. Prompted Chris to be sensitive.
2. Prompted Chris not only to be sensitive, but how to share (out of vulnerability).
3. Gave Chris the courage to do as the Spirit prompted.
4. Gave Chris the words to say.
5. Brought together unique circumstances to His glory.

Coincidences? No. The Comforter, the Helper, our heavenly Companion? Yes. The Holy Spirit is all of those things, and you are not alone as you share His love.

As you consider your challenge in leading your family to be healthy and on mission for God, you will at times feel overwhelmed by the responsibility. Therefore, it is especially important that you understand that you are not the leader, nor the empowerment of the effort. The Holy Spirit is there to guide you.

Jesus said in John 14:15-26 that the Holy Spirit would:
  a. Be your helper
  b. Be with you forever
  c. Be in you
  d. Teach you all things
  e. Remind you of the things of God you already know

This is great news. The Holy Spirit is the source of your strength, your power. It is His glory shining through you. You are a messenger, not a source; you are a conduit, a vessel bearing life-changing news. There is nothing about you that will change or save—it is all Him, His glory, His power, His indescribable mercy. You can take every course known to man in

> *But you shall receive power when the Holy Spirit has come upon you*

sharing the gospel, but if you go forward without the Holy Spirit, it is of no value. This must be regularly and intentionally communicated to your family.

Going in the power of the Spirit leads us to effectively do whatever He has given us to do, no matter the size of the task. Consider Jesus' words in John 14:12 (NKJV), "Most assuredly, I say to you, he who believes in Me, the works that I do he will do also; and greater works than these he will do, because I go to my Father."

He went to the Father so that the Father would send the Spirit. The Spirit indwells the believer, and thus you are empowered. You and your family are on mission for God, and God is right there with you every step of the way.

These truths are related directly to the command to share the gospel in Acts 1:8 (NKJV), where Jesus says, "But you shall receive power when the Holy Spirit has come upon you" right before he says "and you shall be witnesses . . ."

The Holy Spirit in the Believer's Witness
* He empowers us to witness (Acts 1:8).
* He gives us wisdom (Luke 12:12).
* He gives us boldness (Acts 4:31).
* He helps us in our praying (Rom. 8:16).
* He gives us the burning desire to see people saved (Acts 4:29-31).[50]

The Work of the Holy Spirit in the Unbeliever
* The Spirit precedes the witness (Acts 10:1-15).
* The Spirit convicts the lost person (John 16:7-11).
* The Holy Spirit regenerates (John 3:5-6).[51]

You have all the tools you need to share the gospel. But He provides the power to make the tools effective. You are on mission in partnership with the very God of the universe. Go in His strength.

The Basics of Relational/Intentional Evangelism

Andrew and Grace have lived in the same apartment building as Bobby and Joanna for two years. One or the other has asked Bobby or Joanna to attend church at least 25 times. A weak "maybe" is the strongest response they have ever received.

Andrew and Grace have prayed for the couple daily, praying intently and taking them meals through troubled times—like when Bobby's father died and when Joanna was afraid she had cancer. Bobby and Joanna are nice people, but something seems to always be off-kilter. Bobby has had three jobs, Joanna four. Nothing seems to fit.

Andrew and Bobby love baseball, so Andrew has shared several stories out of Christian magazines about big league players who are Christians. Bobby obviously reads them—he comments every time, but always about how well that guy turns a double play, or what a great slider a certain pitcher throws.

Once, Grace actually asked Joanna if she thought she would go to heaven if she died. An embarrassed, flippant answer followed—a clear cue that Joanna did not want to talk about it. Frustrated, Andrew and Grace wonder if they will ever reach Bobby and Joanna, but they are buoyed by the fact the relationship remains, and by the knowledge that it is God's work that actually draws people to Him.

Finally, the big break comes. As is often the case, it comes through hard times. Six months after Bobby's father dies of heart failure, his mother develops a fast-moving cancer. Four months to live, they say. Andrew and Grace visit a visibly shaken Bobby and Joanna. "I don't know how he'll get through it—so soon after his Dad dying," Joanna tells them out of Bobby's presence.

Andrew feels impressed that it is time to be more direct. When Bobby sits down next to Joanna, Andrew says, "I know it's been hard for you, Bobby, and you, Joanna, and it's not looking like it will get easier anytime soon. Grace and I care about you both a lot, and we don't want to step outside our boundaries, but I've got to tell you both that I believe with all my heart that the only way you will make it through this time, and the only way you're going to have stability and joy in life, is to turn to Jesus Christ. Please indulge me long enough to let me explain."

There is silence for a minute, then Bobby says, "Okay, Andrew. Fair enough. We're not really into that, but, you guys seem to have something, and you're obviously sincere. You've been good friends, so we'll hear you out. What about your Jesus?"

Andrew, then Grace shared their testimonies. Bobby and Joanna listened respectfully. Neither accepted Christ that night, but the dialogue was open, and off and on for weeks Andrew would talk to Bobby, and Joanna would quiz Grace. A few months later, just weeks before his mother's death, Bobby accepted Christ. Joanna did the same within days.

Many Christians, maybe most Christians, would not have invested two years of friendship with nonbelievers just for the opportunity to tell them about Jesus. Many Christians, maybe most Christians, would not have been bold enough to lovingly lay the issue on the line as Andrew did. In 1 John 4:19 (NKJV), God's Word tell us that "Perfect love casts out fear."

For Andrew and Grace, God's perfect love overshadowed the fear of what Bobby and Joanna might think of them.

Andrew and Grace were practicing relational, intentional evangelism, a lifestyle of showing the love of Jesus Christ with the specific intent of building a relational bridge over which to share with them the way of salvation through Jesus Christ.

Robinson writes that sharing the gospel "is most effective when done relationally." "Sharing is both relational and intentional," he writes. "It is not either/or; it is both/and. Your spirit and attitude is paramount and should be characterized by love for Jesus and love for the person with whom you are sharing.

You will encounter people at many levels of receptivity

When you love Jesus and you love the person, you will do your best to bring the two together."[52]

That will usually take time, a commodity too many Christians are not willing to spend. "Meaningful relationships are essential to effective sharing," Robinson writes. "Developing a relationship to the point where you can lead someone to Jesus may require an extended time or a brief time. It may take as long as three months or three years, or as few as three minutes, depending on the receptivity of the individual and the work of the Holy Spirit."[53]

You will encounter people at many levels of receptivity. It is important to understand those levels because it will help you be more effective in reaching them. James F. Engel and H. Wilbert Norton developed a scale that will help you understand the readiness of an individual to receive the gospel.

Where someone is on this scale will have a lot do with whether they will respond immediately to your presentation of the gospel. Remember that successful witnessing is sharing Christ and leaving the results to God. You do not fail when you share Christ in the power of the Holy Spirit and they do not make a decision. You may be used to increase someone's receptivity to Christ—in effect, to move him or her along the scale.[54]

	Man's Response
-8	Awareness of Supreme Being but no Effective Knowledge of Gospel.
-7	Initial Awareness of Gospel
-6	Awareness of Fundamentals of the Gospel
-5	Grasp of Implications of Gospel
-4	Positive Attitude Toward Gospel
-3	Personal Problem Recognition
-2	DECISION TO ACT
-1	Repentance and Faith in Christ
	NEW CREATURE
+1	Post-Decision Evaluation
+2	Incorporation into Body (of Christ [Church])
+3	Conceptual and Behavioral Growth
+4	Communion with God
+5	Stewardship
•	Reproduction
•	Internally (gifts, etc.)
•	Externally (witness, social action, etc.)
↓	
ETERNITY	

One of the primary ways of enhancing receptivity is through relationships. The product of a positive relationship is trust. Therefore, relational /intentional training teaches witnesses to gain trust through developing witnessing relationships and then sharing the gospel as God opens the door.

Jesus Christ is the most trustworthy individual who ever walked on this planet. The finest witnessing relationships are based on the lost person being able to see Christ in the witness. It is important to see yourself as a tool in a witnessing matrix. Research shows that the average person hears the gospel eight times before accepting Christ. You do not know if you are number one or number 12. If you lead someone to Christ, you are likely reaping what many others have sowed.

If you sow, someone else may well reap. Realize that you are one of many contact points the Lord will put in the unbeliever's path. An unbeliever may hear about Christ from a neighbor, an uncle, and the person who delivers the paper, the son's baseball coach or an old friend from high school. It is a big picture, and you are important, but just one part of it.

The key is to be faithful to sow the seeds of the gospel and leave the results to God. Be willing and ready to develop relationships and to share with people you will meet just once. In relational/intentional evangelism, remember these simple principles:

- **Invest time**—You will have to make adjustments. You will have to decide to develop relationships and then be sensitive to the Holy Spirit about how to do it.
- **Be sincere**—Love must be sincere. A fake is spotted with ease. See people as individuals in need of Jesus, not objects to conquer for Christ.
- **Be consistent**—You may not spend a lot of time within a particular relationship, but showing consistent love and concern will go a long way. Consistency builds credibility, and credibility is the bridge over which you discuss a person's eternal destiny.
- **Present a clear gospel presentation**—Remember that as you show the love of Christ, you are looking for a clear opportunity to specifically share how a person can become a Christian. Just developing the relationship takes the unbeliever to the threshold of salvation but leaves them separated from God. You may be great at talking to people, but if you never get around to talking to them about Jesus Christ, you're missing the point.

Sharing the Gospel

Don and his family have lived next door to James' family for 11 years. They have had a few cookouts together, helped each other with yard work occasionally on Saturdays. The small talk is always pleasant enough, but James has made it clear from the beginning that he is agnostic and does not want to "talk about religion."

But the gnawing in Don's stomach keeps getting worse. He is under conviction, unable to stop thinking about sharing Jesus with James. The Holy Spirit worked in Don's heart in the past few months, convicting him of his lack of zeal for evangelism. Don has shared at work, in places where he regularly shops—he even led his fast-living little brother to Christ last week.

But James is another case—standoffish, too cool for spiritual things.

Don spends a week mustering up the courage to talk with James. James is a smart man, well read, and holds a Ph.D. in chemistry and works for a chemical plant. "He can probably produce a zillion questions I can't answer," Don figures.

Nothing to lose, though, Don decides. That evening he sees James in his yard and approaches him. He tries to hide his nervousness as he says, "James, I've been living here by you for 11 years, and it occurs to me that I've never had the chance to tell you what I really believe about God. Would you let me do that?"

James stops raking and says, "Sure, why not? Come on over tomorrow evening after dinner."

Don is elated and scared at the same time. He does not know whether to pray all night or study a book on apologetics.

The next night Don goes to James' home. The men sit down alone in the den. For one hour Don tells James how he came to know Christ, how Christ gives meaning to his life, how He encourages and comforts. He speaks of the Bible and how it is God's authoritative Word. James listens politely, virtually expressionless, saying little more than, "Okay" and "Uh, huh."

"That's it," Don says finally. "That's what I wanted to tell you."

James leans forward in his chair. Solemnly, he says to Don, "Okay, I've listened to you carefully. I only have one question."

Don's heart pounds. "This is it!" he thinks. "This is the deep theological question I can't answer. I'm going to blow it!"

"Okay, what is it?" Don says, trying to mask his nerves.

James speaks firmly but in a low tone. "If this is what you've believed all these 11 years you've been my neighbor, why in the world are you just now telling me?"

> *That is what this book is all about: raising your family to follow Christ*

The bottom line is sharing the way of salvation through Jesus Christ. That is what this book is all about: Raising your family to follow Christ. Following Christ means sharing the gospel with those who do not know Him. Jesus said, "Follow me, and I will make you fishers of men" (Matt. 4:19). If you are not fishing, you are not following. You and your family are on mission to be fishers of men. When someone is willing to listen to you, what are you going to say?

The Word of God tells us in 2 Timothy 4:2 (NKJV), "Be ready in season and out of season." There are many ways to initiate a witness of Jesus Christ. It is best if you review several and decide on at least one, clear-cut method that you will use. The FIRM approach, which is simply an acronym to help you remember how to approach someone, is useful with people you do not know:

F— **Ask about family—listen.**
Get to know the person.
Ask questions and be alert.

I— **Ask about their interests—listen.**
Please note who is doing the talking. You will often ask about family and interests and then spend the next 30 minutes listening. This is key to establishing relational bridges over which you can share the gospel. Most people do not care how much you know until they know how much you care. When you listen, you communicate how much you care.

R— **Ask about religion—listen.**
At this point, you need to find out where they are spiritually without being tuned out or they being turned off. Please consider the following options:
- When you attend church, where do you attend?
- Would you say you have come to know Jesus Christ in a personal way or would you say you are in the process?

◆ Do you think much about spiritual things?
◆ Who do you think Jesus Christ was and is?
◆ What are you into spiritually? This question works really well with Generation Xers. They may not be into Jesus, but they are into something spiritually.

M—Share the message.

If their response to your questions indicates that they do not have a personal relationship with Christ, ask for permission to share Christ.

When witnessing to people you know, adapt the FIRM approach. Rather than asking, "Are you married?" ask, "How is your wife/husband?" Another approach is the apology. Say to the individual, "I want to apologize to you. We have known each other for a considerable time, but I've never taken the time to tell you about the most important Person in my life."

Some guidelines for presenting the gospel:

◆ **Choose a method that stresses repentance.**

There are some witnessing booklets that stress God's love and salvation, yet leave out the crucial element of repentance of sin.

◆ **Memorize Scripture in order of presentation.**

This really is not so hard. Many people are intimidated by memorizing Scripture, yet they can list their favorite movie stars and all their movies, or name countless baseball players and their batting averages. Memorizing Scripture is important because you may be in a situation where using a booklet or other written guide is not possible.

◆ **Carry witnessing booklets with you.**

These are easy to leave with people when you do not have time to talk. When you are verbalizing the gospel, you can give someone a booklet and have him or her follow along with you as you make the presentation.

Methods of Sharing the Gospel

There are many methods, both creative and straightforward, for sharing the gospel. There is sometimes debate over which ones are best. Do not get caught up in it. Though one may be better than another in certain situations, most of them work. The key is not how you share but that you share.

I. Preparing and sharing a salvation testimony
A. Items to be included in a 90-second presentation
1. My life before Christ
2. How I realized my need for Christ
3. How I accepted Christ
4. My life since Christ
B. Items to be avoided
1. Sensationalism
2. "Dirty laundry"
3. "Churchy" language

II. Preparing and sharing a recovery testimony
If you received Christ at a very early age, you may want to build your testimony around how God helps you deal with certain issues such as depression, loneliness, and purpose. You may use the following outline or develop one of your own.
A. My life seemed fairly normal until ...
B. I discovered hope and help in Jesus when ...
C. I am glad I have a personal relationship with Jesus today because ...

III. Begin by using a witnessing booklet
A. Advantages
1. It will give confidence to know what to say and when
2. It will assist in presenting the claims of Christ clearly
3. It allows for being brief, staying on the subject, and yet still being sensitive to the Holy Spirit
4. The verses from the Bible are there for quick reference

5. It is both visual and verbal which assists in recall and understanding
6. It provides something for them to take home after the presentation
7. It offers suggestions for growth

B. How to use the booklet
1. Be sensitive to the individual's interest and to the Holy Spirit. As you read the booklet aloud, remember that we are introducing the person to Christ, not just sharing principles.
2. Avoid being mechanical or coming across "canned."

IV. As your witnessing skills sharpen, learn to share a memorized presentation

A. Advantages
1. It allows more sensitivity
2. It is more flexible
3. It is less "canned"

B. The principles are the same as sharing with a booklet.

C. Suggested presentations to learn
1. The NET (North American Mission Board)
2. Faith Evangelism Strategy (LifeWay Christian Resources)
3. Steps to Peace with God
4. Evangelism Explosion (EE)
5. The Roman Road

Healthy families organize and execute around His purpose. Jesus made His purpose clear in Luke 19:10 (NKJV), "For the Son of Man has come to seek and to save that which was lost."

"Lord, may your churches be filled with healthy on-mission families that live your great commandments and fulfill your Great Commission. If this could become a reality, everyone in the world could have an opportunity to respond to Your offer of salvation, and we, as Christian parents would pass the baton of faith in Christ to our children and grandchildren. And Lord, let it begin with my family. Amen."

Steps to Making it Yours

Family Readiness Questions

There is a time for everything. You began by reading the book. Now to help gather your thoughts, review what you have read by answering the Family Readiness Questions.

1. What does it mean to be lost? What are the short- and long-term consequences of being lost?

2. What difference does prayer make in people's lives? What are four specific requests we should pray for the lost (according the chapter)?

3. According to John 14:15, what is the role of the Holy Spirit?

4. What are the commitments a Christian must make for relational evangelism?

5. Name three methods for sharing the gospel. Which ones would you be most comfortable using?

Family Applications

The second step in studying Family to Family *is to discover adjustments through prayer. To help you identify areas in which God may be speaking to you, work through the Family Applications. At the end of each, ask God to reveal any adjustments He wants you to make.*

1. Develop a prayer journal for the lost. Be specific by including names of individuals, their specific needs, and for specific requests for overcoming their "lostness" (e.g., for their eyes to be opened). Monitor your journal regularly and praise God as the people accept Jesus as their Savior and Lord.

2. Write HOLY SPIRIT on the left side of a piece of paper. For each letter, fill in what the Holy Spirit does in people's lives (e.g., hears our

prayers, opens our eyes, etc.). Once complete, make these phrases prayers to God, thanking Him for sending us the Holy Spirit.

3. For each family member, look for ways to make sharing the gospel intentional in two current relationships.

4. Obtain three or four witnessing booklets. As a family, evaluate them and determine which ones your family would like to use. Brainstorm ways to distribute and use them (e.g., leave them with a tip at a restaurant).

5. Make preparing your testimony a family game. Using index cards and markers, write the following headings on the cards: "My life before Christ," "How I realized my need for Christ," "How I accepted Christ," and "My life since Christ." Each family member should have a set of four cards. Spend some time talking about each card, writing in appropriate details for that card. Next, mix up the cards and challenge the family to place them in the proper order. For a greater challenge, place the cards in an envelope and then switch cards. Family members are then arranging someone else's testimony. Once they are in the proper sequence, each family member should read the testimony.

Family Building Activities
The activities allow your family to experience the results of the adjustments you are making. As you select several and carry them out, talk about what God is doing in the life of your family. These activities are not an end unto themselves; they create a teachable moment.

1. Go on a journey to see the lost—shelters, crisis pregnancy centers, the inner city, a mall, an airport, the movies, and a city or state park. After the experience, answer these questions:
   * What are some signs of "lostness" you saw (e.g., empty, searching eyes)?

   * What were people doing to fill the void in their lives (e.g., shopping)?

   * How could your family meet the physical and spiritual needs of the lost people you encountered?

2. Have testimony night over a bowl of popcorn or a pizza. Each family member prepares and delivers his or her testimony. Family members then help one another refine the testimonies to have the greatest impact. Be prepared for questions and concerns, as some family member might not have a testimony. In other words, they might realize during this activity that they have not accepted Jesus as Savior and Lord.

Scripture
The following verses were found in the sixth chapter of Family to Family. *For further application you could allow each family member to choose the* verse or passage that meant the most to them and allow them to tell why.

Luke 19:10	John 16:8-11	Romans 10:1
John 3:5-6	John 17:4	Colossians 4:2
John 10:10	Acts 1:8	1 Thessalonians 5:17
John 12:12	Acts 4:31	1 Timothy 2:1-4
John 14:12	Acts 8:26-39	2 Timothy 4:2
John 14:15	Acts 10:1-15	James 5:16
John 15:26	Romans 3:9-12	

Additional Resources

Bill Bright, *The Coming Revival* (Orlando: NewLife Publications, 1995).

Robert Coleman, *The Master Plan of Evangelism* (Grand Rapids: Baker Books, 1972).

Bill Hybels and Mark Mittelberg, *Becoming a Contagious Christian* (Grand Rapids: Zondervan Publishing House, 1996).

Praying Your Friends to Christ (Alpharetta, Ga.: North American Mission Board, 1998).

Darrell W. Robinson, *People Sharing Jesus* (Nashville: Thomas Nelson Publishing, 1995).

The NET (North American Mission Board)

Faith Evangelism Strategy (LifeWay Christian Resources)

CONCLUSION

A student approaches the speaker at the end of a week of youth camp and says, "I just wanted you to know that I think you are a liar and a jerk." The stunned camp pastor responds with, "What did I do to you?" The young man blurts out, "All week you have been telling us that Jesus is the only way to get to God. Well, that simply cannot be true. My dad is chairman of deacons in our church, chairman of the finance committee, and teaches Sunday School. We live in a neighborhood where no one goes to church, and from the first day I can remember until today, I have never once seen my dad walk across the street to talk to one of my neighbors about Christ. If He were the only way to get to God, My dad would be doing something about it."

So how about your family, will it be committed and consecrated? Or careless and carnal? Will you continue in the pounding surf of activities allowing wave after wave to push and pull your family apart? Or will you get alone with God and your family and discover His purpose and then order your families' priorities around it? At the end of the line will your family be able to say what Jesus said at the end of His life, "I have glorified You on the earth. I have finished the work You have given Me to do" (John 17:4, NKJV).

Your response will probably determine whether you will successfully pass the baton of your faith on to your children. The call of our Lord is loud. The case of the demise of the North American family is alarming. The Word of God makes it clear that the significance of mankind—and thus the family—is to be found in our relationship with God the Father and in carrying out His will by His immense power.

Respond to the call. Join God in His redemptive purposes. Ask God to reveal His dream for your family. Take your family back from the world and pass the baton of your living faith in Jesus Christ to future generations. Be an on-mission family that lives the great commandments and fulfills the Great Commission.

ENDNOTES

CHAPTER ONE

1. From the American Family Association Web site at www.afa.net.
2. Taken from the intro to *The Future of the American Family* by George Barna, copyright 1993, Moody Bible Institute, Moody Press. Used with permission.
3. American Family Association Web site at www.afa.net.
4. Excerpted from *The Little House on the Freeway*, © 1987, 1994, by Tim Kimmel, pp. 17-24. Used by permission of Multnomah Publishers, Inc.
5. From "The Baptist Faith and Message" of the Southern Baptist Convention, Section XVIII, The Family, 1998.
6. Edyth Draper, *Draper's Book of Quotations for the Christian World* (Wheaton, Ill: Tyndale House Publishers, 1992), p. 318.
7. Taken from: *A Father's Reward*, p. 253. Copyright 1998 by Phil Downer. Published by Harvest House Publishers, Eugene, Oregon 97402. Used by permission.
8. Richard Land interviewed by Victor Lee, 8 September 1998.
9. Ibid.
10. Barna, *The Future of the American Family*, p. 107. Used with permission.
11. From *Coming Home: Timeless Wisdom for Families* by James C. Dobson, (c)1998. Used by permission of Tyndale House Publishers, Inc., All rights reserved.
12. Dr. Grace Ketterman, "Christian Psychiatrist and Author Shares Qualities of Healthy Families," Baptist Press, 26 October 1998.
13. Barna, *The Future of the American Family*, p. 103. Used with permission.
14. Fred Lowery, speaking at the 'Wounded Heroes' luncheon, Salt Lake City, Utah, 8 June 1998.
15. John C. Maxwell, *The Success Journey: The Process of Living Your Dreams*, (Chicago: Thomas Nelson, Inc., Publishers, 1997), p. 11.

16. Henry T. Blackaby & Claude V. King, *Experiencing God: How to Live the Full Adventure of Knowing and Doing the Will of God* (Nashville: Broadman & Holman Publishers, 1994), p. 32. Used by permission.

17. Ibid.

18 Draper, *Draper's Book of Quotations for the Christian World*, p. 209.

CHAPTER TWO

19. J. Otis Ledbetter and Kurt Bruner, *The Heritage—How to be Intentional About the Legacy You Leave* (Colorado Springs: Chariot-Victor Publishing, 1996), p. 11. Used by permission of ChariotVictor Publishing.

20. Ibid., p. 237.

21. From the Mennonite Brethren Web site at: http://old.mbconf.ca/mb/mbh3512/mueller.htm

22. Henry Blackaby interviewed by Victor Lee, 18 July, 1998.

23. Mueller, from Mennonite Brethren Web site.

24. Blackaby, interview.

25. Blackaby, interview.

CHAPTER THREE

26. Camille Hamilton and Tom McMinn, *Sharing God's Special Plan with Children* (Atlanta: Home Mission Board of the Southern Baptist Convention, 1992), p. 5.

27. Ibid., p. 8.

28. The 88 percent drop out figure is from Jay Strack's experience among the nation's top student ministry leaders (similar studies varied from 75% to 91%). The second figure is based on Proverbs 22:6 and Jerry Pipes' experience from over 30 years of ministry with students and parents.

29. Howard Hendricks interviewed by Jerry Pipes, 10 December 1997.

30. Hendricks, interview.

31. Hendricks, interview.

32. Phil Downer interviewed by Victor Lee, 11 September 1998.

33. Hendricks, interview.

34. Downer, interview.

35. Ted Elmore, *Praying the Heart of God* (Baptist General Convention of Texas, 1993), p. 44-47.
36. Robert Coleman interviewed by Jerry Pipes, 15 December, 1997.
37. Charles Stanley, from his radio message, 'How to Pass on Our Faith,' 19-20 November 1998.
38. Adapted from an article written by Robert Crosby for *New Man Magazine*, September 1996.

CHAPTER FOUR
39. Donald A. Atkinson and Charles L. Roesel, *Meetings Needs, Sharing Christ Member Book* (Nashville: LifeWay Press, 1995), p. 7. Used by permission.
40. Ibid., p. 50. Used by permission.
41. Adapted from material in *Concentric Circles of Concern* by Oscar Thompson, Used by permission. (Nashville: Baptist Sunday School Board, 1981), p. 22.
42. Downer, interview.
43. Ibid.
44. Adapted from material in *Families Making a Difference* by Kenny Rains, (Memphis: Brotherhood Commission, 1994), pp. 13-48.

CHAPTER FIVE
45. Adapted from material in the *SEE: The Evangelistic Block Party Manual* (Alpharetta, Ga.: North American Mission Board, 1998), pp. 3-4.
46. From the Jesus Video Web site at www.Jesusvideo.org.

CHAPTER SIX
47. Darrell Robinson, *The Doctrine of Salvation*, (Nashville, Tennessee: Convention Press, 1992) p. 8.
48. Ibid., p. 15.
49. *Praying Your Friends to Christ* (Alpharetta, Ga.: North American Mission Board of the Southern Baptist Convention, 1998), pp.16-17.
50. Alvin L. Reid, *Introduction to Evangelism* (Nashville: Broadman &

Holman, 1998), p. 160. Used by permission.

51. Ibid., pp. 161-162.
52. Darrell Robinson, *People Sharing Jesus* (Nashville: Thomas Nelson, Inc., Publishing, 1995). p. 72.
53. Ibid., p. 72.
54. Reid, *Introduction to Evangelism*, p. 188.

To order additional copies of this book or
for information about scheduling
an event with Jerry Pipes

Visit us on the WEB at:
www.jerrypipesproductions.com